September–December 2019

Edited by **David Spriggs** and **Helen Paynter**

GUIDELINES

VOL 35 / PART 3

The Bible Reading Fellowship
15 The Chambers, Vineyard
Abingdon OX14 3FE
brf.org.uk

The Bible Reading Fellowship (BRF) is a Registered Charity (233280)

ISBN 978 0 85746 778 2
All rights reserved

This edition © The Bible Reading Fellowship 2019
Cover image © Thinkstock

Distributed in Australia by:
MediaCom Education Inc, PO Box 610, Unley, SA 5061
Tel: 1 800 811 311 | admin@mediacom.org.au

Distributed in New Zealand by:
Scripture Union Wholesale, PO Box 760, Wellington
Tel: 04 385 0421 | suwholesale@clear.net.nz

Acknowledgements
Scripture quotations from The New Revised Standard Version of the Bible, Anglicised
edition, copyright © 1989, 1995 by the Division of Christian Education of the National
Council of the Churches of Christ in the United States of America. Used by permission.
All rights reserved.

Scripture quotations taken from The Holy Bible, New International Version (Anglicised
edition) copyright © 1979, 1984, 2011 by Biblica. Used by permission of Hodder &
Stoughton Publishers, a Hachette UK company. All rights reserved. 'NIV' is a registered
trademark of Biblica. UK trademark number 1448790.

Every effort has been made to trace and contact copyright owners for material used
in this resource. We apologise for any inadvertent omissions or errors, and would
ask those concerned to contact us so that full acknowledgement can be made in
the future.

A catalogue record for this book is available from the British Library

Printed by Gutenberg Press, Tarxien, Malta

Suggestions for using *Guidelines*

Set aside a regular time and place, if possible, when and where you can read and pray undisturbed. Before you begin, take time to be still and, if you find it helpful, use the BRF Prayer on page 6.

In *Guidelines*, the introductory section provides context for the passages or themes to be studied, while the units of comment can be used daily, weekly or whatever best fits your timetable. You will need a Bible (more than one if you want to compare different translations) as Bible passages are not included. Please don't be tempted to skip the Bible reading because you know the passage well. We will have utterly failed if we don't bring our readers into engagement with the word of God. At the end of each week is a 'Guidelines' section, offering further thoughts about or practical application of what you have been studying.

Occasionally, you may read something in *Guidelines* that you find particularly challenging, even uncomfortable. This is inevitable in a series of notes which draws on a wide spectrum of contributors and doesn't believe in ducking difficult issues. Indeed, we believe that *Guidelines* readers much prefer thought-provoking material to a bland diet that only confirms what they already think.

If you do disagree with a contributor, you may find it helpful to go through these three steps. First, think about why you feel uncomfortable. Perhaps this is an idea that is new to you, or you are not happy about the way something has been expressed. Or there may be something more substantial – you may feel that the writer is guilty of sweeping generalisation, factual error, or theological or ethical misjudgement. Second, pray that God would use this disagreement to teach you more about his word and about yourself. Third, have a deeper read about the issue. There are further reading suggestions at the end of each writer's block of notes. And then, do feel free to write to the contributor or the editor of *Guidelines*. We welcome communication, by email, phone or letter, as it enables us to discover what has been useful, challenging or infuriating for our readers. We don't always promise to change things, but we will always listen and think about your ideas, complaints or suggestions. Thank you!

To send feedback, please email **enquiries@brf.org.uk**, phone **+44 (0)1865 319700** or write to the address shown opposite.

Writers in this issue

Andrew Rogers is Principal Lecturer in Practical Theology at the University of Roehampton in London, where he runs an ecumenical degree programme for students engaged in Christian ministry. He is the author of *Congregational Hermeneutics: How do we read?* (Routledge, 2016).

Pauline Hoggarth was born in Peru and served with Scripture Union in three different roles in the UK and overseas. She is the author of *The Seed and the Soil: Engaging with the word of God* (Langham, 2011).

Steve Hollinghurst is an Anglican priest and the Contemporary Apologetics Officer for the Methodist Church. He is the author of *Mission-Shaped Evangelism* (Canterbury Press, 2010), and writes and speaks widely.

Bill Goodman encourages and enables lifelong learning among church leaders in the Anglican diocese of Sheffield. He has taught biblical studies for various courses and colleges, in UK and overseas.

Steve Walton is a researcher and teacher of the New Testament who serves as an Associate Research Fellow of Trinity College, Bristol. He is an Anglican priest, and has served in different ministries and taught in many universities.

Ernest Lucas has doctorates in both science and biblical studies. After doing biochemical research, he was a Baptist minister and then Vice-Principal and Tutor in Biblical Studies at Bristol Baptist College.

Jenni Williams is Tutor in Old Testament and Dean for Women at Wycliffe Hall, Oxford, and is also Associate Minister at St Peter's Church, Wootton in Oxfordshire. She is the author of *God Remembered Rachel* (SPCK, 2014).

Walter Moberly is a Professor in the Department of Theology and Religion at Durham University. He recently wrote *The Bible in a Disenchanted Age* (Baker Academic, 2018) and is the author of *Ezekiel (People's Bible Commentary)* (BRF, 2009). He is a long-suffering supporter of Sunderland AFC.

Andrew Francis is a URC minister, poet/writer and community theologian. He is also a conference speaker and Sunday preacher. His latest book is *Eat, Pray, Tell: A relational approach to 21st-century mission* (BRF, 2018).

Andy Angel is the vicar of St Andrew's, Burgess Hill. Previously, he taught New Testament in Anglican training colleges and has written various books, including *Intimate Jesus: The sexuality of God incarnate* (SPCK, 2017).

Harriet and Donald Mowat, now in their 60s, have spent their professional lives researching the care of older people and working in clinical practice. Their faith helps them understand better the challenges of the ageing journey.

David Spriggs writes...

How quickly the years run by. It's time to be thinking about Christmas again! Let me share with you some of the 'goodies' we have in store.

Steve Walton brings his stimulating explanation of Luke's gospel to a climax as he takes us through the resurrection stories and the consequences for the disciples. One of the most famous stories in this section of Luke is the walk to Emmaus, which shows that Jesus saw his mission through the Old Testament – and so we as Christians need to pay close attention to it, too.

Helping us to do this is Pauline Hoggarth, who presents the first of her two-part series on Jeremiah. With Jeremiah, we are given glimpses of a man sharing in both the suffering of God and of God's people. Bill Goodman's notes on Ezekiel are such a contrast. Ezekiel's priestly background shapes his testimony to his encounters with God. Like Jeremiah, he is also called to experience the sufferings of God and his people. Jenni Williams provides a fascinating complement to these prophets as she writes on Deuteronomy, a book that reflects the issues of exile and restoration while being rooted in the earlier history of Israel.

Ernest Lucas offers us very insightful human encounters by unpacking the themes that are scattered throughout Proverbs, including friends and neighbours, family relationships, sex and power.

Then comes a short contribution that seeks to explore the links between the Old and the New Testaments. Walter Moberly examines the theme of 'Exaltation and abasement' as it occurs in the Magnificat and how this reflects back on Old Testament passages

Andy Angel helps us think about Matthew's contribution to our understanding of Advent, while Andrew Francis explores some of the scriptural significance of sharing meals together – which itself is a helpful contribution to this Christmas season. Harriet and Donald Mowat's focus is on ageing and family relationships, which are of vital concern to our society.

Steve Hollinghurst offers us a stimulating week on mission in the parables of Jesus, while Andrew Rogers, starting with the Emmaus story, reminds us how hermeneutics is a pervasive aspect of all our writing, speaking, reading and responding to scripture.

This issue is the final one for me as Commissioning Editor. It has been a stimulating privilege to be involved with BRF *Guidelines* in this way for the past few years. I am grateful to all the staff 'in house', who have been so supportive and helpful, to our brilliant and ever-growing team of writers, and above all to all of you who read, respond and apply the scriptures to enrich your leadership, mission and spirituality.

The BRF Prayer

Almighty God,
you have taught us that your word is a lamp for our feet
and a light for our path. Help us, and all who prayerfully
read your word, to deepen our fellowship with you
and with each other through your love.
And in so doing may we come to know you more fully,
love you more truly, and follow more faithfully
in the steps of your son Jesus Christ, who lives and reigns
with you and the Holy Spirit, one God for evermore.
Amen

Seeking hermeneutical wisdom

Andrew Rogers

When tested by a lawyer about eternal life, Jesus responded by asking this hermeneutical question about the scriptures – 'How do you read it?' (Luke 10:26, NIV). Eugene Peterson comments of this exchange, 'Reading the Bible, if we do not do it rightly, can get us into a lot of trouble' (Peterson, p. 81). Actually, sometimes reading it rightly may get us into even more trouble – such as discovering that our neighbour is not who we'd like them to be.

Asking *how* we read the Bible is the business of hermeneutics – the art and science of interpretation. That the Bible needs interpreting is evident throughout the scriptures (e.g. Nehemiah 8:1–8; Luke 24:13–35). Asking how we interpret scripture is also vitally important for Christians who ascribe some sort of authority to the Bible, however that is construed. Church history bears witness to the importance of such reflection (or its lack!). Paul's challenging charge to Timothy to be one who 'correctly handles the word of truth' echoes down the centuries (2 Timothy 2:15, NIV).

Wisdom is needed to discern how the Bible's context and our context speak to each other. It is not just a matter of turning an exegetical handle, important though such issues as grammar, context and genre are. Practical wisdom is needed for assessing the moves we make with scripture as part of our Christian discipleship. Such wisdom is gained through prayer and practice, as well as learning from the body of Christ, both past and present, near and far.

Hermeneutics is a 'standing back' from interpretation to consider what we are actually doing with the Bible. This week, we will be varying how far back we stand in order to get different perspectives on hermeneutical wisdom. Closer up, we will look at Christ as hermeneutical key; the disrupting of vested interests through paying attention to the text and its contexts; and the significance of patterns in scripture for today. Further away, we explore how metaphors *in* the Bible characterise our engagement *with* the Bible; the value of virtue for hermeneutics; and finally how scripture might inform our approach to theological reflection.

Unless otherwise stated, Bible quotations are from the New Revised Standard Version (Anglicised). Author references are to works in the 'Further Reading' list.

1 'He interpreted to them'

Luke 24:13–35

The Emmaus story contains the most explicit reference to interpreting the scriptures in the New Testament (v. 27). For Luke, the story also serves to take up his readers' own stories of being disciples, of their own transformative encounters with Jesus.

The journey begins with Cleopas and his companion walking away from Jerusalem on Easter Day, deep in conversation about all 'these things' that had happened (v. 14). When the unrecognised Jesus comes near (vv. 15–16), his question arrests them and they stop dead in their tracks (v. 17). Out of their sadness, they tell the story of the things and tell it well enough (vv. 19–24), except it doesn't really add up. They don't recognise Jesus or recognise the meaning of the things they are narrating, hence Cleopas' question in verse 18 is somewhat ironic. They are missing the key.

In response, Jesus offers them a masterclass in hermeneutical wisdom (vv. 25–27). To the two, the cross is the dashing of their hopes that the prophet Jesus was 'the one to redeem Israel' from Roman domination (v. 21). The key, says Jesus, is to tell the story with a suffering and then a glorified Messiah (v. 26), if you are willing to do so (v. 25). We are not given the syllabus for this masterclass, but it is evident that interpreting the scriptures (the Old Testament, in this case) requires Christ to unlock its fullest meaning (v. 27). This was indeed the innovation for hermeneutics in the New Testament – that the scriptures were about Christ.

It is possible to pick up some further clues from the passage as to what seeking hermeneutical wisdom may involve. This wisdom needs to be revealed by the Spirit of Jesus, through word and sacrament (vv. 30–32); it is for both head and heart (v. 25); it may mean reprimand and learning to tell 'the' Christian story differently (v. 25); and it will probably require time and attention because it engages with 'all the scriptures' (v. 27), not just selective comfort reading.

Luke places the resurrection at the exact centre of this there-and-back-again journey (v. 23), just as Jesus recentres his disciples' stories on a suffering and glorified Messiah. The outcome is eyes that are opened (v. 31), hearts burning within them (v. 32) and an unplanned journey back to Jerusalem to talk about no prophet but 'the Lord' (v. 34).

2 Beastly authority

Romans 13:1–7; Revelation 13:1–10

Whose interests does an interpretation serve? Interpretative interests need careful examination, especially where questions of power are concerned. The power of governing authorities and those subject to them is the theme of our passages today.

Romans 13 has always been popular with governments for obvious reasons. Two well-established ways of interrogating vested interests are by paying careful attention to the text (to see what it actually says) and listening to all the biblical voices on a given theme (to counter selectivity). There are many other voices in scripture about the authority of government, however, with Revelation 13 being the most strident critique. Letting these two passages talk to each other has been fruitful for many Christians in discerning how they should live in relation to governments good, bad and indifferent.

While governments continue to quote Romans 13 in their propaganda, they forget it wasn't written to them. It was written for Christians living as a powerless minority in the capital city of the mighty Roman Empire. Paul's letter was directed to specific people, places and times; it is not a treatise on church and state relations. It does, however, offer some common-sense wisdom to a Christian community without political power, for whom rebellion or agitation would threaten their very existence. It is carefully framed by chapter 12 and 13:8–14, where 12:21 urges the churches to 'overcome evil with good' and 13:8–10 identifies the distinctively Christian good conduct Paul has in mind, summed up in Jesus' love command (13:9). Paul is treading a fine political, pragmatic and theological line.

Revelation 13 can be read in opposition to Romans 13, except both passages recognise the provisional nature of governing authority (Romans 13:1–2; Revelation 13:5, 7). Such authority is given by God, and power rarely likes to hear of its limitations, hence the subversion and submission in both passages. There is nothing muted about the critique of power in Revelation 13, however, as it identifies the idolatry and blasphemy of human government (vv. 4–5) when it tries to sit in God's place (v. 2). Here, it takes the terrifying composite form of Daniel's four beasts (Daniel 7:1–7). Naming such a beast needs wisdom! In Revelation 13, many scholars identify 666 with Nero Caesar (v. 18). Such critique *and* submission today are borne out of endurance, faithfulness and love (Romans 13:10), even when the authorities turn beastly.

3 Changing our minds

Acts 11:1–18

Do events and characters in biblical stories provide examples for us to emulate today? To put it another way, does this genre of scripture *describe* or *prescribe* – or does it do both? It is probably the book of Acts that raises this hermeneutical question most keenly. Do the events of Acts 10:1—11:18, involving Peter, Cornelius and the Jerusalem church, provide a pattern of how to go about changing our minds on matters of doctrine and practice?

Acts 11:4–17 repeats the events of Acts 10 via Peter's first-person report to his critics in Jerusalem (vv. 2–3). Luke's inclusion of this repetition underlines the importance of these events, which are a turning point in the history of the church. The church starts to change its mind about Gentiles – they can be full members of the people of God without having to become Jews in the process. This change is ultimately due to the Spirit leading the way (vv. 12, 15–16), so the gospel may go 'to the ends of the earth' (1:8). In order for this bigger change to happen, Peter needs to change his mind and practice regarding matters of Jewish law and custom around food (vv. 8–9), association (v. 12) and implicitly circumcision. Cornelius changes from God-fearing (10:2) to accepting 'the word of God' (v. 1) and the Jerusalem church changes enough to be silenced (v. 18).

Is there a pattern here that informs how Christians might change their minds today? Rather than describe *or* prescribe, the story does both in the sense that it can shape our Christian imagination and discernment when facing contemporary questions of change in the church and beyond. The inclusion of the Gentiles is a unique event in the history of the church, but that God makes no distinction between ethnic groups (vv. 12, 15, 18;

cf. 10:34) has much wider resonance. The Spirit's activity is crucial in bringing about this change, as well as constituting evidence of the change being from God (v. 17). This change comes out of prayer (v. 5), leads to conflict (vv. 2–3) requiring accountability and explanation (vv. 4–17) and results in praising God and repentance (who for?) (v. 18; cf. 10:46). Reading the longer story, we see also that the change is in continuity (or even fulfilment) and discontinuity with existing understandings of the scriptures (v. 1, 8–9; 15:22–23). All are significant for seeking hermeneutical wisdom today.

4 Wrestling with scripture

Genesis 32:22–32

How might you picture the way you engage with scripture? The Bible offers some images itself, such as a tree by a stream (Psalm 1:3) or eating and drinking (Jeremiah 15:16; 1 Peter 2:2). The more adversarial image of wrestling in today's passage has fired the imagination of many Christians. Indeed, wrestling with scripture can be a highly appropriate image, since it floors, trips, confronts, circles and resists our holds on meaning and our attempts to 'name' it. Engagement also reveals our vulnerabilities and is sometimes painful.

Today's passage features a turning point in Jacob's life. He is afraid that his brother Esau will kill him, because he deceived Esau in the past, and that's how Jacob's mind works (his name can mean 'grasper'). Jacob fearfully sends his family and possessions across the Jabbok, so that he is alone (v. 24), and it is dark (vv. 22, 26). That is when God chooses to ambush Jacob (and the reader?) as a strange wrestler (v. 24), perhaps as an unexpected response to his prayer earlier in the chapter (32:9–12).

The Bible can be quite strange to us, and there are times when we struggle to see God's face in it. Many things in scripture are not easily grasped, and the struggle to do so (rather strangely) is an irreplaceable part of developing hermeneutical wisdom. The very ambiguity of this passage speaks to this struggle. Does God cheat by putting Jacob's hip out of joint (v. 25)? Does Jacob win (vv. 25–26, 28)? Why does Jacob command God to bless him (v. 26)? Does God lose to win Jacob? As a review of the commentators makes clear, there is no easy resolution to the depths of this text.

Clearly, such wrestling is time- and energy-consuming and the blessing may be hard fought. Wrestling with scripture does mean change, as 'grasper' becomes 'Israel', an incremental transformation to a name that means 'he strives with God' or 'God strives' with Israel (or you and me) (v. 28). It is worth the fight when we see something of Peniel – God's face (v. 30). For Jacob, as he limps off into the sunrise to meet his brother (v. 31), such change tilts towards the New Testament idea of power in weakness (Walter Brueggemann, *Genesis*, 1982, p. 271). Wrestling with scripture may not be an image for every day, but it may get us through the darker nights.

5 Becoming virtuous readers

Colossians 3:5–17

Seeking hermeneutical wisdom is not unrelated to our character. Christ is our wisdom (Colossians 2:3) and, as those whose lives are hidden in him (Colossians 3:3), we have been clothed and are urged to clothe ourselves with the new self (vv. 10, 12). That new self is being renewed in the image of its creator (and Christ is the agent of creation, Colossians 1:16), with its characteristics spelled out in verses 12–14. We might call these characteristics Christian virtues, the shape of which is given throughout scripture, both implicitly and explicitly. This passage is one of the more explicit virtue passages in the Bible; indeed, Tom Wright calls it 'a primer in Christian virtue' (Wright, p. 126). Significantly, the intellect and mind do not appear to be exempt from being clothed in virtue, given the references to knowledge (v. 10), the word and wisdom (v. 16), and doing all in the name of the Lord Jesus (v. 17).

Christian virtue, however, differs from the Greek philosophical tradition as found in Aristotle. In our passage, we find that growth in virtue is directed towards being renewed into the image of Christ (v. 10), where ethnic and status divisions are irrelevant (v. 11). Such virtue is both a gift of God's grace, but also entails growth in character through the hard work of letting go of the old clothes and the wearing-in of the new ones (an allusion to baptism is probable in verses 9–10; compare 2:12; 3:1).

If growing in Christian virtue is about all of who we are, heart and mind, word and deed, then it makes a difference to how we interpret the Bible. Growth in virtue is not only a desired outcome of engaging with scripture, but virtue should also inform that engagement. It is a virtuous circle. As virtues bound up in love (v. 14), what might compassion, kindness, humility, meekness and patience look like when shaping the way we interpret the

Bible? They are clearly more than being nice. Some hints are in the passage: we need humility to 'bear with one another' regarding our provisional interpretative judgements and conflicting interpretations (v. 13); we may want patience for paying careful attention to the text when teaching the word of Christ; and admonishing may need love and other virtues (v. 16). Seeking hermeneutical wisdom means growing in virtues for engaging scripture.

6 Reflecting on reflection

Ecclesiastes 1; 9:7–12; 12:8–14

Theological reflection is about letting life and faith talk to each other. As a process that formalises what many do instinctively, it typically takes the form of a cycle that moves from experience *to* deeper exploration *to* engagement with scripture, doctrine and tradition *to* action. Taking time to reflect theologically on experience in this way calls for hermeneutical wisdom. Today, we reflect on how Ecclesiastes might inform the way we do theological reflection.

Ecclesiastes is a sustained reflection on human experience that is part example and part goad (12:11) to our own practices of reflection. 'Mr Teacher' (*Qoheleth*, 1:1) brackets nearly all of his reflection with his partial conclusion, 'all is vanity' (1:2; 12:8). *Hebel* can be translated as 'vanity' (NRSV) or 'meaningless' (NIV), but the stronger 'absurd' fits the text particularly well (Fox, p. 30). The Teacher sees not just a lack of meaning but a violation of meaning in all that is done under heaven, and names this 'absurd' (38 times!).

For Ecclesiastes, the medium is very much the message. The reflection is driven by its twists and turns and contradictions, and the reader needs to hang on for the experience of the ride. The Teacher does not offer us a systematic reflection but more of a stream of consciousness in which he takes time to explore below the surface of life, on matters such as wisdom (1:12–28) and joy (9:7–9). The book claims to be an exhaustive study (1:13; 12:13) that takes seriously the limitations of human experience, even in the light of faith, and resists the rush to interpretative resolution (see 3:11).

The final conclusion in the epilogue(s), whether it is the author dropping their mask or separate author(s), declares an orthodox determination to 'fear God' despite life's absurdities (12:13–14). With this link to the wider wisdom literature (e.g. Proverbs 1:7), it also points to the critical input of the wider faith community to our theological reflections.

Finally, the 'nothing new' of 1:9 contrasts with the 'everything has become new' in Christ of 2 Corinthians 5:17, though it does not cancel the tension between the *now* of absurdity and the *not yet* of the new creation. Such newness does allow for the possibility of transformation that breaks the wearisome cycle of the 'same old, same old' (1:4–10). It goads us to reflect on how such Christlike newness will feature in our everyday theologising.

Guidelines

- How high a priority are questions of 'how' we read the Bible in your Christian community? Who gets to ask these questions? In what ways can we help each other to grow in hermeneutical wisdom?

- If we understand the scriptures through Christ and Christ through the scriptures, how can Christians read the Old Testament in a way that also is faithful to its original contexts?

- How would you make decisions about legitimate government based on the tension between Romans 13 and Revelation 13 (and other relevant passages)?

- Are you convinced that the story in Acts 10—11 (and 15) provides a pattern for change in the church today? Why or why not?

- The wrestling image is an allegorical reading of the Jacob story at Peniel. Such imaginative interpretations have been part of the church's hermeneutical wisdom for centuries. How would you tackle the possible dangers of such readings that some might argue fly away from the plainer meaning of the text?

- Openness, courage, honesty, faithfulness and confidence have also been suggested as hermeneutical virtues. How might these virtues shape the way you interpret the Bible?

- What other passages of scripture might you find helpful for informing how you go about theological reflection?

FURTHER READING

Richard Bauckham, *The Bible in Politics: How to read the Bible politically* (second edition) (Westminster John Knox Press, 2011).

Zoë Bennett, *Using the Bible in Practical Theology: Historical and contemporary perspectives* (Routledge, 2013).

Richard Briggs, *The Virtuous Reader: Old Testament narrative and interpretive virtue* (Baker Books, 2010).

Michael V. Fox, *A Time to Tear Down and a Time to Build Up: A rereading of Ecclesiastes* (Eerdmans, 1999).

Eugene Peterson, *Eat This Book: The art of spiritual reading* (Hodder & Stoughton, 2006).

Andrew Rogers, *Congregational Hermeneutics: How do we read?* (Routledge, 2016).

Tom Wright, *Virtue Reborn* (SPCK, 2010).

Jeremiah 1—23

Pauline Hoggarth

In 1932, Dietrich Bonhoeffer came to realise that he and his church practised a reading of scripture that was comfortable and accommodating, a reading *for* themselves rather than *over against* themselves. Now, urged Bonhoeffer, they must rediscover a way of engaging with God's word that would interrogate their lives and enable them to live counterculturally, as committed disciples of Jesus in a hostile political and social climate. The prophecy of Jeremiah was one of the texts that Bonhoeffer began to read 'over against' himself and his fellow Christians.

In 1934, in London, he preached about God's unwelcome call to Jeremiah to be his spokesman. The sermon would prove prophetic in terms of Bonhoeffer's own life and his death in 1945: 'This path will lead right down into the deepest situation of human powerlessness. The follower becomes a laughing-stock, scorned and taken for a fool, but a fool who is extremely dangerous to people's peace and comfort, so that he or she must be... locked up... if not put to death' (Bonhoeffer, p. 350).

Over the next two weeks, we will reflect on the carelessly accommodating attitudes to God and his word that were the context in which Jeremiah sought to call his people back to serious listening and response to the Lord: 'The prophets prophesy falsely, and the priests rule as the prophets direct; my people love to have it so' (5:31).

The book of Jeremiah doesn't provide us with an orderly narrative. Intriguing episodes of Jeremiah's life, his inmost thoughts and creative communication are juxtaposed with passages of harsh judgement and suffering expressed mostly as poetry. This is not congenial reading; it severely tests Bonhoeffer's challenge to read 'over against' ourselves. But our times have much in common with the contexts of both Bonhoeffer and Jeremiah. We need urgently to 'ask... where the good way lies; and walk in it' (6:16).

Unless otherwise stated, Bible quotations are from the New Revised Standard Version (Anglicised). Author references are to works in the 'Further Reading' list.

1 Unwelcome summons

Jeremiah 1

'It comes over a person from the outside, not from the longings of one's own heart... The word that... takes us captive... is the... unexpected, forceful, overpowering word of the Lord that calls into his service whomsoever and whenever God chooses' (Bonhoeffer, p. 350).

Some time in 627BC, the 13th year of the reforming king Josiah's reign in Judah, God's unexpected and unsought word summoned a diffident young Jeremiah to a task he immediately questioned. On at least two counts he believed himself inadequate (v. 6). But inadequate is a good place to start when it comes to responding to God. Scripture is full of evidence of his preference for unlikely people for his purposes – men and women who are not confident, not self-sufficient. Moses, Gideon and Mary are among them (Exodus 4:10–13; Judges 6:15; Luke 1:34). Did Jeremiah hope that his timid response might silence God's searing message and close the conversation? Or did he sense that God's intimate knowledge of him (v. 5) probed deeper than all his inadequacies? The text tells us nothing about his immediate response. But in the 40 years or so of public ministry that lay ahead of him, God's word proclaimed through Jeremiah would indeed be dramatically active (v. 10). Jeremiah would often struggle to trust God's promises of direction, provision and presence (vv. 7–8, 18–19), but he consistently resisted pressure, stood firm (v. 17) and faithfully communicated the Lord's unwelcome word.

'What do you see?' (vv. 11, 13): the repeated question to Jeremiah opens another window on God's understanding of what made this young prophet tick. The audio-visual image of the almond branch, with its accompanying pun (Hebrew *shaqed*, 'almond', and *shoqed*, 'watching'), would be a reminder to Jeremiah every springtime that God meant what he said. The vision of the boiling pot, tipped towards the south, towards Jerusalem and Anathoth, Jeremiah's home, was darker. Everyone in Judah was aware of hostile forces to the north. It would be Jeremiah's agonising task to declare the relationship between the approaching disaster and his people's forsaking of God (vv. 14–16).

These two visions sustained Jeremiah throughout his life. They can also sustain us. We need to hold in creative tension our trust in the energy and power of God's word with a realistic acknowledgement of the presence of evil in our world. 'By means of the blossoming almond and the boiling pot we are trained to live with a keen edge of hope and to never be intimidated by evil' (Peterson, p. 55).

2 Imagine, remember...

Jeremiah 2:1–25

Imagination is the capacity to be receptive to images and ideas that are not actually present to our senses. We often underrate the place of imagination in the development of faith and practice of discipleship, giving more importance to propositional, abstract communication. But it's clear that the God who recruited Jeremiah as his spokesman believed in engaging the human imagination to bring about change and response. We have listened in on Jeremiah's 'seeing' of the almond branch, the boiling pot, the fortified city. His receptive imagination has engaged the cogs of his will; we now find him in Jerusalem proclaiming God's message and seeking to expand his community's stunted imagination and selective memory so as to see their situation with God's eyes.

Two powerful images preface this poem: the honeymoon and the harvest offering (vv. 2–3). To sense the shocking incongruity of the bridal metaphor, we need to recall Jeremiah's world at the time. For 57 years, two deeply corrupt kings had ruled Judah. Manasseh and his son Amon were admirers of all things Assyrian (that boiling pot in the north), and had imported into Judah and Jerusalem all the cruelties and hideous decadence of the dominant world power of the time. (Their reigns are described, through different lenses, in 2 Kings 21 and 2 Chronicles 33.) Jeremiah was born during the last decade of Manasseh's reign into a world that could not have been more different from God's reminder of his loving, protective, covenant intimacy with his people, symbolised in the offering to him of the holy harvest first fruits.

From that longing backward look the poem unfolds, relentlessly spotlighting political and faith leaders who are no longer anchored in God, no longer listen seriously to his word, who preside over pick-and-mix religion and shoddy approximations of what is true (vv. 8, 11, 13). We mustn't hurry past these disturbing accusations, but be open to reading over against ourselves, as individuals but also as members of Christian communities, of our societies. God's word alerts us to what these distortions may look like here, today. Who are our gods, the sources of our confidence? Where do we go for easy-access reassurance (vv. 18, 25)? To what extent are we willing to relate the suffering in our society to our forsaking of God? Do we ever consider our own need to repent (v. 23)?

3 God's grief

Jeremiah 3:6—4:4

Jeremiah prophesied during the reigns of five kings of Judah. The first was Josiah (3:6). Son of Amon and inheritor of those 57 years of corrupt leadership in Judah, Josiah was only eight when his reign began. The record tells us that as a teenager he 'began to seek the God of his ancestor David' and that at age 20 he launched reforms that aimed to rid his country of the vile religious practices that had seduced his father and grandfather (2 Chronicles 34:1–7). Six years later, repairs to the neglected temple in Jerusalem that Josiah ordered and financed produced a remarkable find. Hilkiah the high priest discovered the lost scroll of 'the book of the law of the Lord given through Moses' (2 Chronicles 34:14) – probably a core section of Deuteronomy. This rediscovered text would direct Josiah's work of helping his people to become once more a community that lived out God's ways and values. It also shaped Jeremiah's understanding of what God was like.

Deuteronomy called God's people to a relationship of faithful, exclusive, covenant *love* – love of the Lord in response to his love for them and love of others, especially the outsider and the vulnerable (Deuteronomy 10:12–20 is one example of many). Jeremiah's shock tactics remind his audience of God's loving purposes for them (v. 19) and jolt them with images of what they have become – promiscuous whores (vv. 6–10), unfaithful wives (v. 20). The inevitably patriarchal perspective of these texts makes for difficult reading today, alongside the reports that reach us almost daily of widespread, mostly male, sexual misconduct and abuse in all walks of life, but most grievously in churches of every kind and among church leaders.

To read these accusations 'over against' ourselves will involve something different for each one of us. But it must surely include identifying with the pain God feels when we play fast and loose with his love: 'I thought you would call me, My Father, and would not turn from following me' (v. 19). The poet-priest George Herbert (1593–1633) understood at a deep level that the Lord is no passive onlooker of the human condition:

Almighty God doth grieve, he puts on sense;
I sin not to my grief alone,
But to my God's too; he doth groan.

4 Band-aid spirituality

Jeremiah 6:9–30

It is deeply moving to listen to Bonhoeffer's London sermon, as he stands in Jeremiah's shoes and identifies with him: 'Imagine how Jeremiah would have preferred to talk differently – how gladly he would have joined with others in shouting "Peace" and "Well-being!" where there was in fact strife and disaster' (Bonhoeffer pp. 350–60). 'Well-being!' was the complacent Nazi 'Sieg Heil' slogan that Bonhoeffer knew to be a mockery of the truth. He recognised Jeremiah's context of soothing falsehoods, of band-aid solutions applied to the deep wounds of his people (v. 14).

It is sobering to reflect today on our own trafficking in sedative Christianity. A hard-hitting essay from *Sojourners* declares that, 'instead of striving to be a place for divine communion where disciples praise and worship Jesus, churches become infatuated with *accommodation* – making people comfortable, happy, entertained, safe, and content… instead of helping the poor, feeding the hungry, tending to the sick, sheltering the homeless, fighting injustice, speaking for the voiceless, sacrificially giving, and wholeheartedly loving our neighbours (and enemies), churches have become co-opted by secular values and empty content' (**sojo.net/articles/have-churches-become-too-shallow**).

Jeremiah's devastating accusations bring to a close the long section of prophecies that began with chapter 4. The theme is unambiguous: God will unfailingly bring judgement on his careless and indifferent people (4:6, 26; 6:1, 22). Yes, there are glimmers of hope. God will not make 'a full end' of his judgement (4:27; 5:18); there is still the possibility of a return to the ancient paths and the good way (v. 16). But the present reality is 'terror… on every side' (v. 25).

This text alerts us, as western Christians, to our tendency to read selectively, to dismiss talk of invasion and wholesale devastation as being about *others*, other peoples caught up in conflict on the far side of the world. As societies and Christian communities, we are not innocent of any of the wrongs that grieve God and that we have heard Jeremiah so painfully expound. We close our ears; we become indifferent to God's word; we are financially greedy and careless about the ethics of the market; we deal falsely and act shamefully; we are indifferent to God's good ways and spurn his rest for our souls; we keep up religious appearances but act corruptly. And the reassuring refrain continues: 'Peace, peace...'

5 Incoherent

Jeremiah 7:1–15, 27–28

The Jerusalem temple had been the focus of King Josiah's reforms. The rediscovered Deuteronomy had shaped them and Jeremiah's preaching had supported them. So it is a surprise now to find Jeremiah preaching in the same temple an outspoken message about unfinished business and superficial changes. Scholars differ about the circumstances of this sermon. One tradition links it to Jeremiah's temple address around 609BC, at the start of the reign of King Jehoiakim, the second son of Josiah (26:1–2; 2 Kings 23:28–37 tell the complicated story of the succession).

At one level, the reforms have been successful. The people 'enter these gates to worship the Lord' (v. 2). There's a sense of satisfied congratulation as they remind each other that they're in the 'right' place, 'the temple of the Lord, the temple of the Lord...' (v. 4). But Jeremiah perceives a profound disconnect between the complacent buzz of worship and what goes on outside the temple. National leadership is no longer concerned for high standards in public life. King Jehoiakim has returned to the dark ways of Manasseh and Amon and is under the thumb of Pharaoh Neco. As always, it is the poor and vulnerable who are suffering the results of the incoherence of rhetoric and reality (vv. 5–6) in public and religious life.

Nearly 700 years later, Jesus recalled Jeremiah's words when he confronted the commercialism and the religious control freaks in the same temple: 'You have made it a den of robbers' (Mark 11:17; compare v. 11). The apostle Paul wrote soberly to young Timothy about the incoherent behaviour that was likely to emerge in times of political and economic distress: 'holding to the outward form of godliness but denying its power' (2 Timothy 3:5).

Our church communities tend to use terminology that plays a similar role to those temple slogans of Jeremiah's day – the equivalents of 'This is the temple of the Lord.' The familiar language allows us to identify, feel comfortable, feel safe (v. 10). We know we're 'OK' if we can recognise and use it. But the same language can also exclude people and, worse, it can be incoherent with our lives beyond the slogan zone, when we trust in 'deceptive words to no avail' (vv. 8–10). This tragic disconnect between what the Christian community says and what it does is reflected in global headlines – not just about child abuse but about attitudes to migration, conservation, gun control and the nature of truth.

6 'My poor people...'

Jeremiah 8:18—9:16

There are seven passages in the book of Jeremiah that have been described as 'confessional'. They open up with extraordinary honesty the inner life of the prophet, his communication with God when he is not out in the public arena calling his people to repentance. 8:18—9:3 provides our first opportunity to listen in on Jeremiah's prayer life and it is a complete contrast to the threatening terrors of the previous passages (8:4–17) and to what follows (9:4–16).

But whose voice or voices are we listening to? It's confusing; we move between accusations attributed to God (9:2b–3) and expressions of pain and longing in the face of 'the cry of my poor people' (8:19), 'the hurt of my poor people' (8:21), 'the health of my poor people' (8:22) and 'the slain of my poor people' (9:1). 'It is likely that the pathos of God and of the poet here are indistinguishable' (Brueggemann, pp. 91–92). Jeremiah has come a long way from his initial rejection of God's call to deep identification with God's inmost heart. In shocking contrast, we also hear the voice of the people themselves expressing a tough, business-as-usual attitude (8:19) and impatience with God's rescue timetable (8:20). There is a tragic incongruity between this public insensitivity and the grief of God and his prophet.

Scripture records that weeping is a characteristic of God's faithful prophets and leaders. Ezra, Nehemiah and Paul wept with and for their people (Ezra 10:1; Nehemiah 1:4; Philippians 3:18). Jesus wept over Jerusalem's blindness to 'the things that make for peace' (Luke 19:41–42).

The question of whose voice we are hearing surely troubles us most in the voice of God/Jeremiah longing 'that I might leave my people and go away from them!' (9:2). A Muslim friend once said to me, 'You Christians are so glib about grace. You believe forgiveness is easy for God. We take sin much more seriously.' Maybe the unbearable thought that God might long for some lodging place in the desert to get away from us will strengthen us to reject Bonhoeffer's 'cheap grace'.

Guidelines

- On the two visions that God provided for Jeremiah at the outset of his ministry (Jeremiah 1:11–13), Eugene Peterson writes, 'By means of these visions he kept his balance and sanity and passion in the theatre of God's glory and through the holocaust of human sin… He kept his grip on reality, never shutting his eyes to the ugly evil around him, never cynically dismissive of the glory exploding around him' (Peterson, pp. 54–55). To what extent do you find yourself able to maintain Jeremiah's balance? Where do you see signs of hope today? Where do you find the most disturbing evidence of evil?

- It would be helpful at this point to take time to read the histories of Jeremiah's times in 2 Kings 21—25 and 2 Chronicles 33—36.

- To what extent has the exploration of these opening chapters of Jeremiah expanded and/or changed your understanding of what God is like?

- Dietrich Bonhoeffer's discovery of 'over against' reading of scripture changed the direction of his life. Do you recognise similar turning points in your own experience of interacting with God's word? What have they been?

- God's invitation in Jeremiah 6:16 was turned down. But what if we welcome it, meditate on it, turn it into prayer and loving, grateful response?

1 What's in a covenant?

One of the most exciting and helpful ways of exploring the Genesis-to-Revelation narrative is through the lens of *mission* – the mission of God to bring back to himself and bless all the peoples of the earth. Within this story, 'covenant' is a crucial recurring theme. It speaks of the initiatives God takes to enter into unique relationships characterised by blessing, both with individuals – Noah, Abraham and David – and with an entire people, through his covenant with Israel at Sinai (Exodus 19:5–8), renewed when the people entered the promised land (Deuteronomy 29:10–15). God's vision for these covenant relationships is always the extension of his blessing beyond one family or ethnic group. His promise to Abraham is that 'you will be a blessing… in you all the families of the earth shall be blessed' (Genesis 12:2–3). Solomon, dedicating the temple, prayed for foreigners who might visit, 'so that all the peoples of the earth may know your name and fear you' (1 Kings 8:43).

In an earlier message, Jeremiah had declared his people's return to faithful covenant relationship as the *condition* for God's blessing of the nations (4:1–2). Now, in what commentators identify as his fourth public address, Jeremiah focuses in the most outspoken terms on the long history of his people's failure as faithful covenant keepers, their indifference to God's communication (v. 8) and their collaborative idolatry (vv. 9–10).

Reflecting on what God's covenants show us about his work of mission, Richard Bauckham declares that 'the church is always caught up in the movement of God's purpose from one to all… So the church should be the community from which the blessing of Abraham, experienced in Jesus, overflows to others' (*Bible and Mission*, Baker Academic, 2003, p. 49). When the Christian community betrays its purpose and fails to bear witness in the world to God's holiness and goodness and desire to bless, are we prepared for the anger of those close to us – for Jeremiah, his fellow citizens in Anathoth (v. 21) – if the Lord should call us to expose such betrayal? And how shall we understand God's word to Jeremiah not to 'lift up a cry or a prayer on their behalf' (v. 14)? This is the second time that he has been forbidden to intercede for his people (7:16). But can we understand this as a word for us, today? The apostle John, who wrote so passionately about the transforming nature of relationship with God, also contemplated the awesome possibility of silence in the face of stubborn sin (1 John 1:6–10; 5:16–17).

2 A severe obedience

Jeremiah 12

'How often… they must have wished that they did not have to keep on threatening, warning, protesting and bearing witness to the truth! But necessity is laid upon them. "Woe to me if I do not proclaim the gospel!" God, why are you so close to us?' (Bonhoeffer, p. 352). The young pastor's outspoken complaint, as he reflected on the courage and suffering of his fellow Christian rebels in 1930s Germany, finds echoes in Jeremiah's breathtakingly honest second lament. This is nothing less than an accusation against God for presiding over a universe of inverted morality, in which people who do evil prosper and the treacherous thrive while paying lip service to the Lord. The rejection and threats of his Anathoth neighbours have caused an emotional maelstrom in Jeremiah – fury at the prosperity and ease of people who are dismissive of God's reality (v. 2), longing for revenge (v. 3) and grief over the destructive drought (v. 4). Most distressing of all is what Jeremiah seems to experience as the unfeeling rightness of God (v.1), combined with the kind of intimate understanding ('God, why are you so close to us?') that is both comforting and unnerving when it probes deep into a fierce desire for revenge (v. 3).

At the start of Jeremiah's ministry, God had met his doubts and inadequacy with reassurance (1:8, 19). Now, as his prophet faces death threats on the streets of Anathoth, we expect promises of God's protection and provision. Instead, we rock back on our heels to hear his analysis of a worsening situation and no relief (vv. 5–6). It's been hard going on the plain; now the Jordan jungles lie ahead for Jeremiah. No one can be trusted. This is hard to deal with. Surely our faithful endeavours for God will be met with reward? Surely those agonised questions about right and wrong deserve a response? But, like Job, Jeremiah receives no direct answer about the success of wicked people (Job 38—41). He is required to walk by faith, not by sight.

Maybe what Jeremiah took away from God's unwelcome answer was some assurance that in a worsening situation (vv. 7–13), the Lord could imagine him braving the Jordan jungles and running with the horses. 'To serve such a God is not merely an act of dedicated loyalty and intentional decision-making. It is, rather, an inescapable destiny once one has grasped a certain reading of reality. The prophet is compelled to speak without any assured reward' (Brueggemann, p. 120).

3 Cloth and clay

Jeremiah 13:1–11; 18:1–12

We've already watched Jeremiah responding to the Lord's vivid images of life as his prophet (1:11–13, 18). Now, we look on as God takes other familiar items and situations in Jeremiah's life and proposes alternative, prophetic understandings of them.

Never again would Jeremiah put on the familiar male waistcloth without remembering that new one, paid for, briefly worn, then taken to the riverside (either the Euphrates, 500 miles from Jerusalem, or Parah, close to Anathoth), buried among the rocks and dug up 'after many days' – ruined and good for nothing (13:7). The pristine new linen, intended for intimate wear, has become useless, muddy and stinking, a shocking metaphor for God's corrupted people. Destined for beautiful intimacy with him, they have rejected their true identity and become worthless. It's unclear whether this acted parable was for Jeremiah alone or for a wider public.

We can only guess at the chronology of these episodes of Jeremiah's experiential learning with God. His ruined linen and what it symbolised surely left him depressed and grieving. The Lord's invitation to watch the potter at work appears at first to introduce a new, hopeful note. In the potter's skilful hands, the 'spoiled' pot (the same Hebrew word as the 'ruined' loincloth – 13:7) can be reworked 'into another vessel, as seemed good to him' (18:4). It is the potter's sovereign control over the clay that Jeremiah seems at first most aware of. The clay itself is inert in the potter's shaping hands (18:6). But two conditional scenarios push the boundaries of the analogy. 'If' is a crucial word in the language of covenant (Deuteronomy 7:12); here, it opens the possibility of repentance and disaster averted (18:8) or the opposite (18:10). Unlike the inert clay that has no will of its own, the people are free to respond to God or to resist his shaping. The note of hope is so powerful, the option of change so clear and persuasive (18:11), the possibility of reshaping into goodness and beauty so tangible (18:4) that the

26

people's abrupt response comes as a shock (18:12). It seems that long-term stubborn resistance to God ends up limiting our capacity for repentance and change: 'It is no use' (18:12) are some of the saddest words in the book.

4 I sat alone...

Jeremiah 15:10–21

'What we do in secret determines the soundness of who we are in public. Prayer is the secret work that develops a life that is thoroughly authentic and deeply human' (Peterson, p. 108). This is a countercultural claim in our times, when the message is so often that what we do in our private life can be kept conveniently compartmentalised from our public role. One of the marvels of the book of Jeremiah, as we have already witnessed in earlier 'confessional' passages (8:18—9:3; 11:18–23; 12:1–6), is the access it provides to the prophet's inner life, the often outspoken conversation with God that seems to have been the constant context for his gruelling work of public proclamation and the painful fallout from it. The public ministry of Jesus had similar deep roots in private, and sometimes conflicted, prayer (Mark 1:35; Luke 6:12; 22:41–42).

Jeremiah denounced the deceptive sedative messages of the establishment spokesmen ('Peace, peace'; 'temple of the Lord'). But he took no pleasure in doing so. He struggled with his identity as 'a man of strife and contention' (v. 10) and with the loneliness that came with authentic identification with God's ethical standards (v. 10b) and adamant threatening word (v. 17). Once more, God's response seems unfeeling, matter-of-fact (v. 11) and, worst of all, seems to say that Jeremiah's suffering is pointless, that the iron and bronze of his unpopular preaching will ultimately be powerless against the iron of the northern invader (vv. 12–14).

One of the measures of our relationship with God is surely the boldness and truth of our praying. Would we have the courage to come back to the Lord with Jeremiah's imperatives? Remember me, visit me, take revenge for me, protect my life (v. 15): such daring petitions can only be the result of a deep relationship, already tested over time and poured out now in a profoundly moving confusion of joy and pain, delight and anger, loneliness, angry doubt and outspoken accusation (vv. 16–18).

God's response can be heard at several levels: a surprisingly conditional 'yes' to his troubled prophet that seems to demand even more from him

(v. 19); a resounding assurance of commitment to the messenger of the sender of the message – 'I am with you' (vv. 20–21); and, possibly, as words of comfort to the exiled Jewish community. 'What Jeremiah knows in his prophetic vocation, Israel comes to know in its exile, where it also senses abandonment' (Brueggemann, p. 150).

5 Fire in my bones

Jeremiah 20

Jeremiah battled all his life against superficial reform, shallow responses to the word of God. King Josiah's purification programme, carried out in response to the discovery of the 'book of the covenant', was all about dramatic action – breaking, burning, cutting down – that seems not to have touched the heart of the matter: the true state of people's relationship with God (2 Kings 23:1–27). They had 'gone on building the high places of Baal to burn their children in the fire' (19:5). Jerusalem's civil and religious leaders had watched the prophet smash a clay pot in one of the city's gates and heard God's word to them: 'So will I break this people and this city, as one breaks a potter's vessel, so that it can never be mended' (19:11). When Jeremiah repeated the message of terminal destruction in the temple, one official took drastic action (vv. 1–2).

It can be sobering, when we read scripture, to ask where we 'find ourselves' in the narrative. It's one of the ways in which we can learn to read God's word 'over against ourselves'. With whom do we identify? As we witness this confrontation between prophet and priest, might we consider whether, like Pashhur, the high priest's deputy, we are drawn to what Brueggemann calls 'official truth' and are closed to the alternative, prophetic understanding of reality that Jeremiah so disturbingly and insistently proclaimed? Pashhur was surely only doing his duty, dealing appropriately with dissent in a public place, ensuring a smooth operation. He probably genuinely struggled to believe that God would act against the temple, the institution that stood for him and his purposes.

On Jeremiah's part, there was no compromise. After a painful and humiliating night in the stocks, he confronted Pashhur in the harshest of terms (vv. 3–6) and experienced an emotional reaction that took him into deepest darkness (vv. 7–18). Jeremiah's seventh and final 'confession' seems to have spoken particularly powerfully to Bonhoeffer, especially his experience of the inescapability of God (vv. 7, 9): 'Not to be able to get away from God is the constant disquieting thing in the life of every Christian' (Bonhoeffer, p. 352). Jeremiah's short burst of praise isn't a neat last word, and it doesn't bring comfortable resolution (v. 13). His lament closes bleakly (v. 18), bearing true witness to the cost of faithfulness to God's word and to the astonishing honesty of the Bible.

6 Despair and hope

Jeremiah 21; 23:1–8

Jeremiah had proclaimed God's word through the reigns of four kings – two of them brief interludes of a few months and, with the exception of Josiah, characterised by the corruption that Jeremiah had consistently condemned. In 597BC, King Nebuchadnezzar of Babylon invaded Judah for the first time and carried into captivity the fourth of these kings, Jehoiachin (also called Jeconiah, 24:1). He then appointed Jehoiachin's uncle as a vassal king in Jerusalem, changing his name to Zedekiah. Zedekiah would be the last king of Judah (597–586BC).

We find him a frightened man, ruling over an uneasy city that echoes to the sounds of Chaldean siege beyond the walls (21:2). Zedekiah 'did what was evil in the sight of the Lord' (2 Kings 24:19); nevertheless, in a desperate situation, he and his religious advisors still acknowledged some connection between political events and the reality of God. Irony of ironies, they actually seek out Jeremiah as a last resort to 'inquire of the Lord' on their behalf (21:2). The words imply a deliberate searching after and listening to God, as in Isaiah 55:6. The prophet gives them short shrift; it's no good now harking back to God's wonderful deeds in previous generations. The powerful language that described the Lord's actions in support of his people in the past now describes his actions *against* them and therefore in support of Babylon (21:5, compare Deuteronomy 5:15). Commentators discern four answers to the king's request: two offer no hope (21:3–7, 13–14); the second holds out the possibility of hope in exile (21:8–10); the third offers a fleeting vision of authentic repentance and transformation (21:11–12). None of the responses can have brought comfort to Zedekiah, whose life would end in horrific circumstances (39:1–7).

Jeremiah 22 and 23:1–8 focus on the nature of monarchy and of individual kings – the joy and health that accompany righteous leadership

(22:2–4), the hopelessness of living under oppressive and greedy kings/shepherds (22:13–17; 23:1–2) and finally the glowing promise of a king of kings who will practise righteousness and make it possible for his people to 'live in safety' (23:6). King Zedekiah had asked Jeremiah about the possibility of a 'wonderful deed' for his people (21:2). The promises of 23:7–8 will not be fulfilled in continuity with the past ('it shall no longer be said') but in a new work of God that must inevitably include the experience of exile.

Guidelines

- Priest and scholar Raimon Panikkar once wrote, 'Worship is, above all, truthfulness.' As you look back on Jeremiah's three 'confessions' or laments that we have meditated on this week (11:18–23; 12:1–6; 20:7–18), to what extent do you find it helpful, even liberating, to consider their truthfulness as 'worship'?

- In an interview, Walter Brueggemann was invited to identify some present-day prophets. He listed some well-known names, insisted that many prophets are local with no public profile and defined them as men and women who 'are attentive to the concrete costs of dehumanisation and are convinced that there is a larger, holy purpose to life that cannot be reduced to vested interests… They reimagine the human process according to the holy purposes of God' (Brueggemann, *Like Fire in the Bones*, Fortress, 2006, p. 208). Who would you identify as prophetic voices in God's purposes today, and why?

- Vivid metaphors and experiential learning were an integral part of Jeremiah's developing relationship with God – from the blossoming almond to the potter's wheel. Take time to reflect on the extent to which your capacity for imagination has helped you to grow in faith and responsiveness to God.

FURTHER READING
Dietrich Bonhoeffer, *Works*, Volume 13 (Augsburg Fortress, 2007).
Walter Brueggemann, *A Commentary on Jeremiah: Exile and homecoming* (Eerdmans, 1998).
R.K. Harrison, *Jeremiah and Lamentations* (Tyndale Press, 1973).
Eugene H. Peterson, *Run with the Horses: The quest for life at its best* (InterVarsity Press, 1983). There is a revised 2009 edition.

Mission in the parables of Jesus

Steve Hollinghurst

One of the distinctive traits of Jesus' teaching is the use of parables. Those of us within the Christian faith can be immune to the impact the parables had on their first hearers, due to our familiarity with them. Yet, within our increasingly non-religious society, this is changing.

I am reminded of a conversation I had with a man visiting a stall I was helping run at a Mind Body Spirit fair. He asked me without prompting if God could forgive someone regardless of what they had done. As part of my response I said, 'Jesus told a story about this in which there was a father who had two sons...', as I guessed he had never heard the story. When I spoke of the younger son asking for his inheritance, he exclaimed, 'The bastard! Fancy treating your old man that way!' He had got the point of the terrible behaviour of the younger son in much the way Jesus' hearers would.

This illustrates something we will explore further: that the very nature of parables is evangelistic. In addition to that, several of them in their content address mission issues. It is for good reason that Luke has the parable of the sower in chapter 8, before the twelve are sent out in chapter 9. It is also, as that last point suggests, worth noting how different gospel writers arrange Jesus' parables in different contexts, making their general principles address different situations.

My hope is that by exploring mission in the parables of Jesus, we may be inspired not only to understand better Jesus' teaching on mission, but also to find new ways of using these stories in our evangelism.

Unless otherwise stated, Bible quotations are from the New Revised Standard Version (Anglicised).

1 The use of parables

Often Jesus' use of parables is explained as taking illustrations from everyday life to make his teaching accessible. Yet here, Jesus says he uses parables to ensure people who are not within the circle of his followers don't understand. They are presented more as riddles to baffle than as illustrations to educate. Bob Mayo, in his book *Ambiguous Evangelism* (SPCK, 2004), reports on research into how teenagers process images to discern their meaning. Some images had very obvious interpretations. These were quickly identified and then accepted or rejected according to the young people's existing views. Ambiguous images, however, were challenging; they needed wrestling with to work out what they were saying. It was therefore these images that could awaken new insights. I think Mayo is right to realise that many of Jesus' parables work the same way. That they are not easy to grasp is what gives them their impact; they create in their ambiguity the possibility of seeing the world in a new way, from the perspective of the kingdom of God.

The very nature of a parable, and not just its content, is evangelistic. We live in a culture in which we can no longer assume religious knowledge and also one in which story and narrative are increasingly more important than factual statements in seeking to convey ideas. The use of parables in evangelism makes sense in such an environment. Sometimes, the parables Jesus himself told will have such an impact. It may also be that we create new missionary parables for our day inspired by Jesus' example. As Mayo shows, these may be images and not just words.

Matthew quotes from Isaiah 6:9–10, the call to send Isaiah to speak to the people. In the Greek Old Testament here quoted, the people have hardened their hearts and will not hear God's message that they turn and be healed. In quoting this, Matthew offers us the possibility that those hearing Jesus, like the people of Isaiah's day, will have hardened hearts and not respond; indeed, this section of Jesus' teaching follows his rejection by the Pharisees in chapter 12. However, there is another possibility. Others may be moved, as the disciples were – and turn and find healing.

2 The sower

Luke 8:1–8, 11–21

Luke frames the parable of the sower between an account of the women who followed him and supported the twelve financially and the saying about his mother and brothers and sisters being those who do as he teaches. Luke wants to emphasise that the true disciples are shown by their fruitfulness. In this context, the parable contrasts the seeds that bear no fruit with the ones that produce an abundance of it. Jesus is answering the question, 'Why do some reject Jesus and others welcome him?' The first thing to note is that this is due to the soil and not the quality of the seed. The seed of the gospel can produce fruit in anyone, anywhere, but the 'soil' has to be ready for it. Jesus tells the disciples how, for some, the devil takes away the word, so they never come to faith; for others, there is a surface acceptance that cannot face testing; and for others, the cares of the world choke faith as it grows.

However, Jesus' audience may have been struck by another detail. Seed is expensive; you don't waste it on soil that is not capable of producing fruit. Now, when we know it is people's lives we are talking about, we might respond that you do not know where the fruitful soil may be, and so God's word is given to all generously. It is only when we see fruit that lasts that we know where the good soil was. This certainly is good guidance for us in our witness; we only ultimately know where the receptive people are by offering all the word and calling all to follow Christ. If Jesus calls us to share God's word generously, regardless of the soil, it is worth pondering that a good farmer seeks to prepare the soil for sowing. Sometimes in our mission there may, I believe, be a phase where the work of God is for now to prepare the soil. Often, when we 'sow' and see a harvest, it may be because someone else has already helped prepare that place or person. This also should encourage us when our work in God's mission appears fruitless; we do not know what harvest another will reap from what we have done.

3 Wheat growing secretly

Mark 4:26–29

This short parable follows Mark's version of the parable of the sower and builds on the image of sowing the word as a metaphor for mission and evangelism. First, it reminds us that it takes time to see the fruit of our work in God's mission. The seed needs to germinate and grow and mature. Indeed, with the previous parable in mind, it is the fruit that lasts which we are looking for, not seed on what proves to be the rocky ground, which germinates and sprouts but has no root and so withers away.

In Matthew 28:18–20, often called the 'great commission', Jesus tells the disciples to make other disciples among all nations. This is not just about people receiving God's word with joy and acceptance but persevering in it. My fear is that sometimes we look for the numbers who respond to judge the success of missionary activity, when this is only the beginning of someone's conversion. This may then encourage us to seek a quick response to God but then fail to do the work of enabling someone to become a disciple and bear fruit that does not wither away.

This parable also reminds us that it is God who makes the growth happen, in secret, in ways we do not understand. Indeed, the seed we sow is also given us by God and not something of our own making. If we are sowers and tenders of soil, and nurturers of those who grow, it is God's secret work that enables that seed to be fruitful. It is easy sometimes to think successful mission is about the right training, method or materials. Such things may indeed make us better at what we do, but without the work of God they will achieve nothing. Remembering this will keep us both humble and prayerful as we play our part in God's mission.

Finally, we also need to discern when it is time for the harvest. Because we do not know what God is doing in secret, we wait attentively for the fruit to appear. Then, when the harvest time comes, we seize the moment to gather it in. There are moments like that too in mission, when people are now ready to follow, and it is time to call them because the work of God is bearing fruit.

4 Seeking the lost and rejoicing when they are found

Luke 15

Luke 15 has three parables about seeking the lost and rejoicing when they are found. The first of these, the lost sheep, also appears in Matthew, but in the very different context of valuing children. Here, Luke adds two further parables unique to his gospel. The Pharisees complain that Jesus is welcoming tax collectors and sinners, and the parables are addressed to them. However, as Jesus was teaching 'tax-collectors and sinners' (v. 1), it is likely they were also present. These 'sinners' are the 'lost' in each parable. Rather than staying away from such people, as the Pharisees did, God goes out to find even one who is lost. Indeed, the Pharisees should be rejoicing that such people are coming to listen to Jesus because this shows God is rescuing them and bringing them home. This rebuke of the Pharisees is also an affirmation of the tax collectors and sinners. They were welcomed by Jesus, and God rejoices to have them with him. Compared to being ostracisaed by the Pharisees, this was indeed good news.

The emphasis of the probably misnamed 'parable of the prodigal son' is on the refusal of the older brother, modelled on the Pharisees, to welcome the younger home. The father's actions in looking out for his lost son, running to meet him and then largely ignoring his son's prepared speech, show his delight in having him home. He is immediately restored as a son and heir, signified by putting upon him the father's robe and ring. As my friend at the Mind Body Spirit fair realised, this is especially astonishing after the younger son has in effect wished his father dead by demanding his inheritance. The older brother, however, thinks his father's love needs to be earnt by good service and resents it being given freely to the wasteful younger brother, to whom he refers as 'your son' and not 'my brother'.

A few years ago, I reviewed a book by Christians involved in mission in nightclubs. Many reported that other Christians criticised them for being in such sinful places. Jesus' message is that there aren't any 'no-go' areas in God's mission. God wants to seek out the lost wherever they are. Further to this, the hard-heartedness of the older brother reminds us that love, compassion and empathy should be our motivation in seeking them. They, too, are our brothers and sisters.

5 Salt and light

Matthew 5:13–16

Immediately before the parables of the salt and the light, Jesus ends the beatitudes by telling the disciples to rejoice when they are persecuted, because that is how the prophets were treated. The disciples, like the prophets, will be witnesses for God, a theme continued in these parables.

There is much debate about what kind of salt Jesus was referring to and what exactly is meant by the salt losing its flavour. Part of the problem is that salt had many uses. Salt also can't lose its flavour; it is chemically incredibly stable. While some have argued that salt was impure and so could lose its flavour, I think Jesus and the disciples will have known this did not happen. Indeed, these two parables are clearly a pair, and the idea that salt could not lose its flavour is matched by the city on a hill that cannot be hidden. Similarly, the idea of hiding a light under a bushel is not seriously being contemplated. The point is that the disciples cannot fail to be witnesses to God rather than them being exhorted to be so.

A further problem is the Greek word *moranthe* being translated as 'lose its flavour'. This word in other instances is translated as 'become foolish'. However, salt and light were metaphors used by rabbis for the wisdom of the law of Moses. Such a metaphorical use would fit Jesus' teaching, which goes on to talk about the fulfilling of the law and the need to surpass the righteousness of the Pharisees in doing so. The disciples' lives being salt and light witnesses to that kind of righteousness.

Jeremiah 31:33 speaks of a time when God will write the law in people's minds and hearts, a prophecy the author of Hebrews 10 believed was fulfilled as a consequence of the death of Jesus. This is a work of the Spirit through God's grace, not something we can do. Jesus is telling the disciples, and us, that we cannot help but be witnesses to Jesus because of what he does in our lives.

I often like to remind those I teach of the idea that 'they may be the only Jesus people ever meet'; their lives are a witness. It is good that this is ultimately down to what God does – and not our own effort.

6 The mustard seed and the yeast

Luke 13:18–21

It is easy to judge the impact of mission by the number of those who respond to an evangelistic message. If the parable of the sower warns us that it is not converts but lasting disciples we should seek, these two parables tell us that mission that starts small may have great consequences. Indeed, we can note from the gospels that Jesus is far more concerned with teaching his disciples, and especially the twelve, than he is with counting as followers the 5,000 whom he miraculously fed. This points to one of the key elements of the growth of the early church. Jesus did not create a mass movement but a small group he had given time and attention to. In doing so, he equipped them, with the aid of the Spirit, to do the same. A great public evangelist can indeed enable many to respond, but of itself this only adds to the church. Jesus, on the other hand, built a small church, one able to expand not simply by addition, but exponentially as each member brought others to faith and discipled them to do the same. Enabling individual Christians to bring a small number to faith is far more effective than having a few who can evangelise large numbers. Indeed, if every Christian in Britain led someone to faith every five years and enabled that person to do the same, it would take only 25 years for everyone to become a disciple.

If great outcomes from small beginnings is the common theme of these parables, each has its own emphasis. While mustard plants can grow to nine feet, they're not really suitable for birds to nest in. Again, Jesus takes something and exaggerates it to show just how fruitful God's mission is. The image is of a tree so massive that birds, probably a metaphor for Gentiles, come from all over to make their home in it. This picture becomes reality in the global spread of the kingdom and shows the kingdom welcoming in people of all races and cultures. By contrast, the yeast is not an image of welcoming in but of going out. The small work of God in the disciples becomes something that, when it gets into the world, can totally transform it. This also reminds us that the goal of mission is not just about people coming to faith, but the coming of the kingdom that transforms the world.

Guidelines

- It has been suggested that Jesus' use of parables is a form of 'ambiguous evangelism', challenging people to adopt a different worldview. From your experience, is that reflected in the faith journey of others or yourself?

- In explaining the parable of the sower, Jesus likens the different soils to different states people may be in when they hear God's word. I have suggested that a wise missionary might 'prepare the soil before sowing the seed', so that as much soil as possible is ready to produce a good crop. How might one prepare people to be more receptive to God's word? Can we protect them from the devil snatching the word away, or the cares of the world choking it, or the 'rocks' in their lives stopping it take root? Why might these be issues for some people and yet seemingly not for others? What part might faithful ministry, counselling, care and support play in opening people to receive God's word and 'bear fruit' and how much is this the work of God's Spirit over time? Do you know of people or places that used to be unresponsive to God's word that are now being transformed by it? If so, why do you think the situation has changed? How might such questions inform the part you play in God's mission?

• If a small group of disciples who help enable others to be disciples is the secret of the exponential growth of the early church, why does this not seem to be happening in many churches today? How might we enable such growth to happen?

• Many of Jesus' parables are about the coming of the kingdom. If the kingdom of God were to come in your community, what would it look like? What would need to be transformed for that to happen? What part might you or your church play as the 'yeast' working to help that happen?

• How do you feel about the idea that 'you may be the only Jesus some people meet'? How might that relate to Paul's image of the body of Christ? Might it be better to view this idea as being about the witness of the Christian community rather than solely the individual? If you look at your life, what signs are there of God's work that others might see? Many of us respond to such questions by fearing the answer is 'not much'. If so, might we be underestimating what God has done in our lives?

FURTHER READING

Jerram Barrs, *Learning Evangelism from Jesus* (Crossway, 2009).

Robin Gamble, *Jesus the Evangelist* (Kingsway, 2010).

Steve Hollinghurst, *Mission-Shaped Evangelism* (Canterbury Press, 2010), chapter 7.

Bob Mayo, *Ambiguous Evangelism* (SPCK, 2004).

Ezekiel 1—24

Bill Goodman

How can you make sense of life when your world falls apart? Is it possible to survive the trauma and find a different, more positive future? When disaster strikes, where is God – and can you hold on to faith in God?

Five years have passed since the invading Babylonians forced Jerusalem to surrender in 597BC. The conquerors uprooted many leading figures and their families from their homeland, marching them to exile in Babylon (2 Kings 24:10–17). Now Yahweh, the God of Israel, calls one of these exiles as a prophet, to speak into the chaos and bewilderment of their new situation. God's words through Ezekiel offer a key to understanding the disaster that has overwhelmed their nation. Born out of this crisis, the messages preserved in the book of Ezekiel provide an extreme, vehement response aimed to shake up those who hear them and to guide them towards a better future.

Ezekiel's words and images are sometimes similar to those of Jeremiah, a fellow prophet who remained in Jerusalem at around the same time. Ezekiel's visions also influenced later Jewish mysticism and apocalyptic writings, such as the New Testament book of Revelation.

The book may have been edited over time, perhaps by Ezekiel's disciples; but it gives us some clear indications about the author. It opens abruptly with the phrase 'In the thirtieth year' (1:1), perhaps a reference to Ezekiel's own age. As a priest (1:3), he would have expected to begin his duties in the Jerusalem temple at the age of 30 (compare Numbers 4:3, 30). Instead, he finds himself in distant Babylon with the other exiles. At this poignant moment of disappointment, God speaks to him and calls him.

Ezekiel is an unusually vivid book: 'I looked' (1:4, 15); 'I fell on my face' (1:28); 'I sat there among them, stunned' (3:15). This is the only prophetic book written almost entirely in the first person. We enter into the prophet's personal experiences of awe, fear, distress, revulsion, agony and hope, as described in his own words.

Biblical quotations are from the New Revised Standard Version (Anglicised) or else the author's own translation.

1 Unexpected and astonishing: God arrives

Ezekiel 1:4–28

After a brief introduction to the prophet and his community, we are abruptly ushered into a spectacular visionary experience, described in vivid, impressionistic language. A kind of breathless bewilderment comes across in words that are sometimes disjointed, even ungrammatical. Some of the details may puzzle us, but let's grasp the overall impression.

The vision abounds with movement. A storm wind blows in, energised with flashes of fire and lightening (vv. 4, 13); strange creatures are seen darting to and fro, their multiple wings beating furiously (vv. 5–11); as the creatures fly, we see wheels turning within other wheels and lifting off the ground, moving and then halting (vv. 15–17). Animated by a mysterious 'wind', 'spirit' or 'breath' (vv. 12, 20–21) and drawn by mysterious divine creatures, the chariot is not limited to earthly roads but able to soar though the skies.

Finally, the prophet risks raising his eyes further, to see if he can glimpse the one who is being conveyed in this astonishing vehicle. Opaque language abounds, giving a sense of deference in trying to describe what can never truly be seen or described. We are shown something like a throne, with a seemingly human figure seated on it (v. 26), amid the dazzling brightness associated with a revelation of God (Exodus 19:16–20; Psalm 18:7–14). Finally, we glimpse 'the appearance of the likeness of the glory of Yahweh' (v. 28).

An earlier prophet saw a vision with some similarities (Isaiah 6); yet that throne seemed firmly fixed in the Jerusalem temple. Now Ezekiel sees a throne that is mobile, conveyed on a chariot; the figure seated on it is not limited to Jerusalem, but can visit and meet his people anywhere. This God of the whole earth is free and unrestricted. The same awesome Yahweh God who met his people at Mount Sinai now comes to them again – even here, in Babylon, their place of exile and despair! The God who has brought judgement on his people has not deserted them.

Like an overture for a symphony, this vision sets the tone for the book that follows. A glimpse of the rainbow (v. 28) brings a reminder of Yahweh's earlier promise of covenant grace after the overwhelming judgement of the flood (Genesis 9:12–17) – a hint of the message to come through Ezekiel in the chapters that follow.

2 A bittersweet calling

This life-changing encounter with the majesty of God prompts Ezekiel to fall face down before the royal presence (1:28). But he hears the divine voice addressing him personally and experiences the mysterious 'breath' or 'spirit' raising him to his feet (2:2). He is not to grovel in the dust, but to hear and respond to the word of Yahweh, who is 'sending' him (2:3–4). This affirmation and assurance of God's presence is not simply a mystical gift upon which the prophet can rest and find comfort. It is also a call and a commissioning for service. Perhaps he had gone to the river on that particular day to reflect and grieve about his lost calling to serve as a priest in Jerusalem; now suddenly, he finds himself given a very different responsibility.

In the surreal fluidity of this visionary world, the prophet experiences Yahweh feeding him a scroll, which he eats. God's words taste deliciously sweet, yet the message on the scroll is less than appetising (2:10), as is the briefing which God now gives to his messenger. The 'people of Israel' to whom Ezekiel is sent are 'a rebellious house' (2:3, 5, 7). Speaking to people with whom he shares a common language and culture will prove more difficult than preaching to foreigners (3:5–7)! These early exiles, from the upper classes of Judean society, are probably hoping for a swift return home to their former positions of wealth and privilege. Ezekiel's message – that the exile will not be short, and that rebellious Jerusalem will be captured again and this time totally destroyed – would not be well received by them. But Yahweh will hold Ezekiel to account: he is responsible for delivering this hard-hitting message (see 3:17–21). If people then ignore it, they will only have themselves to blame.

'The hand of Yahweh was on me' (1:3; 3:14). Ezekiel feels bitterness and boiling anger, probably about the tough assignment given to him by God; returning to his community, he sits 'overwhelmed' or 'appalled' for days. He is very human, as emphasised in the way Yahweh repeatedly addresses him as 'son of man', which simply means 'mortal' or 'human one'. But he senses God holding, directing and toughening him up (3:8–11). The name which his parents gave him ('Ezekiel' means 'May God strengthen') is turning out to be more appropriate than they could ever have imagined.

3 Silent proclamation

Ezekiel 3:22—4:17

From the start, Ezekiel's preaching style is vivid and visual. Initially, he is told to stay at home, tied with ropes, saying nothing apart from specific occasions when the Lord Yahweh gives him a word (3:24–27). Strange behaviour for a prophet! Perhaps this general silence is to indicate Yahweh's displeasure, or that Yahweh has no more to say to his people.

Next we see the wordless prophet taking what comes to hand at home – a brick, earth and a frying pan – to construct a model of the city of Jerusalem under siege. In this dramatic mime, he himself takes the role of Yahweh: not inside the city, defending it, but outside with the attackers. Ezekiel takes meagre amounts of water and bread baked on a fire of dung, using these to emphasise the hunger and thirst that will be experienced in the besieged city as time goes on. He lies down for periods of time (perhaps day after day, or simply for a brief period each day), to visualise the length of God's punishment on his people for their incessant sin. After this, he symbolically cuts and divides his hair (5:1–4), while later we watch him digging through a wall and going out shouldering baggage, a picture of Jerusalem's walls being broken through and the leaders and people led out into exile (12:1–16). Then we find him trembling as he eats, in order to convey his people's anxiety (12:17–20).

Some might say Ezekiel's preaching style is creative, perhaps playful; others have called it eccentric. Recent Freudian and psychological readings of the book attempt to diagnose a supposed unstable mental condition in the prophet. A more enlightening approach is to notice some of his biblical peers: other Old Testament prophets also go in for dramatic 'acted oracles'. Thus Isaiah walks around 'naked and barefoot' (Isaiah 20), Jeremiah smashes a pot (Jeremiah 19), Ahijah tears a new coat into twelve pieces and gives ten of them to Jeroboam (1 Kings 11:29–40). A prophet may choose drama as one way to catch the attention of the crowd and even to embody the message in the everyday world. In Ezekiel's case, these sign-acts within his own home seem to have continued over a long period, perhaps attracting a regular stream of visitors.

4 Shocked and shocking

On occasion, Yahweh prompts his silent prophet to speak out. He turns towards his distant homeland and proclaims 'to the mountains of Israel' (vv. 2–3) – the high places traditionally used for worship, where people are worshipping local fertility gods (sometimes alongside, or intermixed with, worship of Yahweh). Yet Ezekiel remains in Babylon, as do his hearers. If they are hoping for a swift return home to 'business as usual' in Judea, they need to think again; the prophet is showing them that more judgement is still to come on their unrepentant homeland. To help get this across to them, God sends them a similar message by letter from Ezekiel's contemporary Jeremiah in Jerusalem (Jeremiah 29).

Ezekiel's favourite word for 'idols' is distinctive, suggesting a shapeless lump; it is similar to the word he used for 'excrement' in chapter 4. It seems that he is deliberately offensive, as if to say 'these are not real gods, but simply disgusting lumps of...' At times, biblical prophets use shock tactics, seeking to shake people out of blindness or complacency and to convey how deeply offensive their behaviour is to Yahweh. (For other examples, see Jeremiah 2:20–25; Hosea 1—3; Revelation 17:1–6.)

In proclaiming violent judgement here (see also 5:13–17), is Ezekiel – and the God for whom he speaks – being cruel and vindictive? It might sound that way to us, living secure and distant from the crisis which Ezekiel's people faced. We need to notice that neither Yahweh nor the prophet wishes disaster upon his people. Indeed, Yahweh speaks personally of being 'crushed' (v. 9; or 'shattered') by Israel's unfaithfulness – there is deep pain alongside God's fury. Despite this, Yahweh refuses to destroy his people completely (vv. 8–9). God's aim and longing is that his people 'shall know ['acknowledge'] that I am Yahweh' (v. 7). This key phrase, heard three more times in these verses (vv. 10, 13–14), is repeated more than 70 times in various forms throughout the book. The Hebrew word 'know' used here indicates committed relationship, sometimes intimacy. Restoring a covenant relationship with his people is at the heart of Yahweh's purpose and actions.

5 Not at home

Ezekiel remains confined to his house and exiled far from home – yet free in his mind and spirit. As he sits with the elders of Israel before him (perhaps they sense God's authority in this eccentric prophet), a figure appears to him – instantly recognisable as the one he had seen on the throne in his earlier vision (1:27). That free, mobile God is on the move again – and taking Ezekiel with him. In the surreal world of a further vision, the prophet finds himself hauled away by the hair, transported across a thousand miles back to Jerusalem.

Set down by Yahweh in the holiest place of his people, the Jerusalem temple, Ezekiel is shown what is really going on there. In the gateway stands an idol, most likely a statue of Asherah or Astarte, the Canaanite goddess, consort of the high god El; this provocative image was probably presented to worshippers as Yahweh's wife (v. 5). Moving further into the holy spaces, Ezekiel finds himself in a creepy, dark room where those who should know better are engrossed in some other foul worship, perhaps of Egyptian animal deities (vv. 10–11). Emerging into the daylight of a courtyard, he finds some women mourning what was probably a Babylonian deity, one believed magically to bring seasonal rain to refresh the parched crops by rising from the dead (v. 14). Finally, Ezekiel's vision brings him into the inner court, as close as one could go to the central building representing Yahweh's presence. Here he finds men turning their backs (and backsides) towards the holy of holies and bowing instead in worship to the sun (v. 16) – which was revered by the Babylonians and others as one of the most powerful gods.

The extent of the insults is deliberate and astonishing. In Yahweh's house, it seems, every kind of deity is being honoured – except Yahweh! People are 'putting the branch to their nose' (v. 17), probably an offensive gesture similar to giving someone the middle finger in our culture. They also oppress the weak with violence – something Yahweh finds equally offensive.

Ezekiel is shown all this to help him understand the reasons behind the judgement which will come on Jerusalem. God is not unfair or vindictive; rather, he has been repeatedly provoked to 'jealousy' and 'anger' by his rebellious and unfaithful people (vv. 3, 5, 17).

6 God's reluctant departure

As his visionary journey in the Jerusalem temple continues, Ezekiel senses the imminence of God's judgement on the sinful, wayward city (chapter 9). Yet those living there seem oblivious to this, not least the local leaders (vv. 1–3). Their proverb about the cooking pot is obscure; it might be expressing complacent confidence or gloomy pessimism. Either way, the prophet is called to challenge them, turning their own proverb against them. Yet he does not relish this task, expressing horror when one of these officials drops dead (v. 13): will Yahweh now totally abandon his people?

In response, this free and sovereign God surprises Ezekiel once again – this time with vivid promises of hope. Yahweh has not given up on them. He promises to meet his scattered people in exile and then to bring some of them home to their own land of Israel. More amazing still, he will soften their hard hearts, put a new spirit within them and restore their committed relationship with him (vv. 16–20). These glimpses of renewal will re-emerge in more glorious detail later in the book.

Before that hope can emerge, the immediate crisis must be faced. When the divine Spirit first set Ezekiel down from his visionary flight into the Jerusalem temple, the first thing the prophet noticed there was the reassuring presence of 'the glory of the God of Israel… like the vision that I had seen in the valley' (8:4). But as the extent of the idolatry and corruption in the temple has been unveiled to him, so he has observed God's awesome chariot begin to move away from the centre of the temple complex towards one of its gates (10:18–19). God has been marginalised, rejected, in the very place that was built to express his presence among his people. The people there have been driving Yahweh out (8:6). As the chariot rises and moves, fiery coals of divine judgement emerge from beneath it. Finally, Yahweh does the unthinkable: the divine glory leaves the temple and the city completely (vv. 22–23). But it stops on the Mount of Olives just to the east of Jerusalem – perhaps hesitating, still reluctant even now to leave? Perhaps waiting to see what will happen next?

The prophet, meanwhile, finds himself suddenly 'returned' to Babylon, released from the visionary world. His task now is to explain to his people what God has been saying and doing.

Guidelines

Does anything in particular from these opening chapters of Ezekiel catch your attention? If so, reflect on it and see if it resonates with your experience in some way.

Here are a few further pointers:

What is God like?

- Ezekiel's visions of God in chapters 1—3 and 8—11 are dominated by an overwhelming sense of divine glory, majesty and holiness. How does that fit into your own understanding of God? As Christians, we also treasure our understanding of Immanuel, God with us, God who comes among us in the incarnation. Can we hold that in tension with Ezekiel's vision? In the book of Ezekiel, Yahweh God comes and speaks to the prophet – then through the prophet to the people around him (and finally, in turn, to us today).

- The divine chariot-throne also emphasises God's mobility and sovereign freedom. What does that mean for us today? Can we see God as the God of the whole earth, present and active everywhere? Are there places, people or even parts of your own life where you would not expect God to turn up and reveal himself?

Exile

- Exodus and exile are two crucial, formative events in the Old Testament: one a triumph, the other a nightmare, both brought about by God. Does the exile experience that we glimpse in the book of Ezekiel speak to us today – as communities? As churches?

- How does God meet us in our own experiences of disobedience and repentance, of crisis, trauma and loss? Perhaps we and others we know can give testimony to this, in ways that can help build faith and resilience.

Humanity

- Yahweh repeatedly addresses the prophet as 'son of man' ('human one'). Being reminded of our humanity and frailty is important for all of us, not least those called to Christian leadership. How shall we acknowledge our humanity and weakness – particularly if God seems to be giving us a difficult calling which requires toughness when faced by people's resistance?

Knowing God

- One of the book's key repeated phrases is 'they shall know that I am Yahweh'. Underlying the prophet's shock tactics and his strident condemnations of idolatry is this deeper purpose. What kind of relationship does this covenant God seek with human beings? How shall we relate to the awesome and holy God revealed in this book?

1 Desperate for security

Ezekiel 13

Ezekiel challenges others who, like him, claim to be prophets. He may not be questioning their sincerity, acknowledging that they speak 'from their heart' (v. 2); his charge is that nonetheless they are wrong, self-deceived. To help make his message memorable, he plays on words: *nabiim* (prophets) can be *nabalim* (fools) (v. 3).

Some of the details Ezekiel mentions are obscure. First, he challenges a group of men and refers to a wall. Perhaps this group has been reassuring people that Jerusalem remains secure from any enemy behind its solid defences; surely God's holy city can never be overwhelmed by foreign invaders: the idea is unthinkable! But these prophets are effectively plastering over the cracks, whitewashing over messy truths. They fail to recognise that the real defence the city relies on – the presence of Yahweh – is no longer in place; Yahweh has departed and joined those who will attack the city. These voices proclaim 'peace' (v. 10): something people long for and want to hear. But there can be no peace when people deny reality (v. 16). Back in Jerusalem, his contemporary, Jeremiah, has been preaching a very similar message (Jeremiah 23.9–22).

Next Ezekiel confronts a group of female prophets (vv. 17–23). He has no gender-related issue regarding their ministry, standing in the wider Old Testament tradition which affirms the prophetic roles of women such as Miriam (Exodus 15:20), Deborah (Judges 4:4) and Huldah (2 Kings 22:14–20). Ezekiel's concern focuses on these women's promotion of wristbands and veils, probably designed to give magical protection from harm to the wearer and/or give them power to harm other people. In doing this, perhaps under the umbrella of the worship of Yahweh, they entangle ordinary people and benefit from doing so. As with the male prophets, the heart of the matter is people's desire for security; as with Jerusalem's walls, the solution is not to design more elaborate and impressive-looking defences, but to look to Yahweh in repentance and faith.

Both the female and male prophets use their own imaginations (vv. 3, 17). Imagination is a God-given gift, to be used as part of loving God with all our 'mind' (Mark 12:30). But it needs to be aligned with God's revelation; otherwise, it may lead into deceptive flights of fancy.

2 Messing with sacred stories

Ezekiel 16:1-22

Have you ever heard this vast chapter (or the somewhat similar chapter 23) read aloud in church? Few of us have, for good reason. It evokes lewd images of sexual depravity and extreme violence. The language used is so shocking and coarse that most of our translations tone down its offensiveness. Here we see prophetic shock tactics at their most extreme. How must it have felt for a priest's son, who was concerned to have undefiled lips (4:14), to deliver such a foul message?

Like many before and since, Ezekiel's people have stories that they hold dear: stories about the past which shape their worldview, giving them identity, security and hope. You tamper with these sacred stories at your peril; Ezekiel deliberately does so. He radically reworks their history, to subvert their conviction that they have been treated unfairly by Yahweh and must soon be allowed to return home. Ezekiel focuses on Jerusalem, the city which his hearers in exile revere as a guarantee of God's favour towards them.

The prophet's version of history makes no mention of faithful patriarchs or Moses leading people to freedom or the glory of Jerusalem during the reigns of David and Solomon. Instead, he reminds them of their roots among idolatrous foreigners (v. 3) and depicts their beginnings in the image of an unwanted, abandoned baby (vv. 4–5). This story is all about God's love and lavish generosity in saving and raising this people (vv. 9–14) – and how they, having flourished through this patient covenant love, then spurned it (v. 17). They have repeatedly sought security, not in the love and protection of their adoptive father, but in alliances with other nations and worshipping other gods – even to the horrific extent of child sacrifice, a practice found in some neighbouring cultures and forbidden by Yahweh (vv. 20–21; see Deuteronomy 18:9–12; Jeremiah 32:35).

In Ezekiel's fluid allegory/metaphor, their rescuer now becomes a loving husband, from whom they turn away and instead choose prostitution; again and again he calls them 'whore' (vv. 15–17). This behaviour is not forced on them, but their own free choice, which has turned into an addictive, insatiable promiscuity with multiple partners. The prophet declares that the entire community of Yahweh's people is a lascivious whore – a particularly shocking message for the leading men to whom Ezekiel preaches (e.g. 14:1–3).

3 Worse than the worst, yet still loved

Ezekiel 16:44–63

Ezekiel's radical reworking of Israel's sacred history continues. To further his point, he now conjures up two 'sisters' for Jerusalem: Sodom and Samaria (v. 46). For his hearers, both cities would be beyond the pale, notorious for idolatry, alliances and corruption. (The sins of Sodom which he spells out here might surprise us: not sexual ones, as in Genesis 19, but instead pride, gluttony, decadence and lack of commitment to the poor and needy – vv. 49–50.) The prophet's message could not be more shocking: 'Your sins', he declares, 'are even worse than theirs were' (vv. 48, 52). Such is the extent of the idolatry and unfaithfulness of Jerusalem over the years.

Just when Ezekiel's verbal hammer blows might pummel the hearer down towards total despair, he suddenly surprises again, with an unexpected twist: 'Yet I will remember my covenant with you' (v. 60). Despite Jerusalem's provocation, which is leading to its imminent destruction under God's judgement, somehow there is still hope. Five times in the closing verses we hear that Yahweh's covenant commitment to his people remains; this covenant vow of a loving husband has not been forgotten and will be re-established. The God who rescued them still longs for his people to 'live' (16:6). Knowing Yahweh is the promised outcome; in spite of everything, forgiveness somehow has the final word (vv. 62–63).

Many readers today find this chapter profoundly disturbing. Some ask whether it portrays God as an abusive husband: all the guilt is loaded on to the female character, while the husband subjects her to public stripping and extreme mob violence (see especially 16:37–43). The offensiveness of the scene rightly revolts us. It is crucial to remember that we are reading the symbolic language of an allegory, framed in terms of an ancient culture which is not our own. The language is deliberately chosen for maximum shock effect, designed to jolt people who are blind or indifferent to the nature of their spiritual and political unfaithfulness. But the power of this vivid imagery is undeniably dangerous and could be misused by some who try to validate abuse. Men who hear these words are called to see themselves as the unfaithful wife in the story, not as the husband. This is not an account of a human marriage; it does not sanction sexual or marital abuse.

4 Choices and responsibility

Ezekiel 18

'The parents have eaten sour grapes, and the children's teeth are set on edge' (v. 2). This proverb seems to have been popular among the exiles of Ezekiel's time. It might mean 'One generation makes mistakes, and the next generation suffers the consequences. That's just the way things are.' (Leading to fatalism and despair: 'There's nothing we can do to make a difference'.) Alternatively, it could mean 'Past generations committed the sins, but it's the present generation who are being punished for them. That's not fair.' (Leading to rejection of responsibility and a victim mentality: 'Blame others, blame God, blame anyone except us.')

Ezekiel rejects this kind of thinking, insisting that each generation is accountable to God and needs to make the right choices. (The 'you' in this passage is plural, indicating that he is speaking to the people as a whole.) Will the current generation be realistic about its need to repent? He gives a series of cameo examples, illustrating what 'righteousness' – a right response to God – looks like. Active goodness is required in religious practice (v. 6a), private morality (v. 6b) and especially the public arena of social and economic relationships (vv. 7–9).

But if 'a child shall not suffer for the iniquity of a parent' (v. 20), how can this be reconciled with Exodus 34:6–7 (also Exodus 20:5), where Yahweh speaks of 'visiting the iniquity of the parents upon the children'? Exodus says that actions have consequences that do affect subsequent generations; for example, if one generation turns to idolatry, their children and grandchildren will be affected and may also become guilty of that sin. But Ezekiel insists that those children should not be punished for the offences

50

of their parents (as happened in some legal systems). Nor should those children avoid their own responsibility to make the right choices. Ezekiel rejects blame-shifting. Each generation is responsible for its own actions: it cannot simply blame the previous generation with a shrug of the shoulders and avoid taking action.

The good news is that complete forgiveness is possible, no matter how serious the sins (vv. 21–22) – and that Yahweh is compassionate, life-giving and life-restoring, not vindictive (vv. 23, 32). There is also a hint of an inner transformation of the heart and spirit which is needed, a theme which will re-emerge in more detail later (v. 31; see 36:24–27).

5 Lament for leaders

Ezekiel 19

Occasionally, the writer of this book surprises us by setting aside the customary prose, with its lengthy and meticulous attention to detail. In its place, we suddenly encounter poetry similar to that found in other prophetic books, with concise, vivid imagery that needs slower, more reflective reading. Certain aspects of the meaning are initially unclear; biblical poetry sometimes puzzles us with ambiguity, teasing the imagination into thought.

This poem explains itself as 'a dirge for Israel's leaders' (vv. 1, 14). A dirge (or lamentation) is a song expressing grief at someone's death (e.g. 2 Samuel 1; also much of the book of Lamentations). So Ezekiel's initial audience would wonder which leaders the song has in mind. The first one it depicts looks so promising – yet is cut short (vv. 3–4), a reference to King Jehoahaz, carried off to Egypt after the defeat and death of Judah's King Josiah. Next we glimpse Jehoiachin, who reigned only a few months before surrendering and being taken off to Babylon with Ezekiel's community (vv. 5–9).

Poets sometimes use imagery in fluid ways. Israel, initially depicted as 'a lioness' giving birth to cubs (v. 2; compare Genesis 49:8–9), now suddenly changes into 'a vine' producing various branches (v. 10; compare Isaiah 5:1–7). Its beauty, strength and fruitfulness are coming to an end. Jerusalem's current leadership, under king Zedekiah, will also end up overthrown and uprooted into exile. He will be responsible for the nation's final downfall and will not be succeeded by another king – the regime will suddenly come to an end (vv. 12–14). Here is the poem's punchline.

Like other prophets, Ezekiel highlights the importance of leadership, not least in the effect it has on others. Power, pride and idolatry are the temptations that can be the downfall of those who have seemed and perhaps felt invincible. When leaders do fail, there should be no perverse or malicious delight in the outcome; the purpose of a dirge is to express grief.

6 Grief without mourning

Ezekiel 24:15–27

What was it like being married to Ezekiel? Being uprooted and dragged off into exile with the Jerusalem elite must have been a nightmare in itself. But then came his erratic and alarming visions as well as his eccentric behaviour and abrasive messages laced with offensive language, not to mention his ongoing refusal to speak, alienating the two of them from the wider community and perhaps from each other (we don't know how much he spoke at home). How his wife felt about their marriage, we can only imagine. But we are given a glimpse of his feelings for her. Yahweh refers to her as 'the delight of your eyes' (v. 16), a term of intense attraction and affection (also found in Song of Songs 5:16 and Hosea 9:16). This brief, poignant phrase is all we know of her and of their life together.

One day, news spreads around the community of exiles: Ezekiel's wife has suddenly died. In the accustomed way of that culture, people gather at his house to express their sadness and support. But to their amazement, they find him not bare-headed, dishevelled and weeping, as expected, but washed and dressed, going about his normal business, declining to touch the customary food which they have kindly brought. Baffled and offended, they must wonder at his apparent callousness.

Many of Ezekiel's guests no doubt realise from experience that there must be some message about God being expressed in this latest example of bizarre behaviour. Sure enough, it comes. Soon, the prophet says, they will all hear unthinkable news: that 'the delight of their eyes' – the glorious temple back home in Jerusalem – has been desecrated and destroyed by the Babylonian army (vv. 21, 25). This news will prove so devastating to them that the shock will leave them paralysed, unable even to express grief in the customary manner.

Although shattered at his wife's death, Ezekiel was forewarned about it shortly beforehand by Yahweh. So his refusal to mourn for one on whom he looked with such delight is done in obedience to Yahweh's strange command and at great personal cost, in order to convey another vivid message. He is also given a glimpse of a different future: when news of the city's fall reaches them in a few months, his time of silence will end – and he will have new things to say to his people on Yahweh's behalf.

Guidelines

What has caught your attention in reading Ezekiel this week? Revisit those verses and pray into whatever God may be saying to you through them.

Some further pointers:

True and false prophets
- Ezekiel reminds us that those who claim to bring God's word to people can sometimes be wrong, even sincerely wrong. As we read this, do we instinctively want to identify ourselves among the true prophets? If so, we need to acknowledge that sometimes we may be the misguided ones, getting God's message wrong or partly wrong.

Offensiveness
- The offensive nature of some of Ezekiel's preaching expresses the offensiveness of idolatry to Yahweh. Do we share that sense of outrage at idolatry today? Should we?

- When challenging people to turn away from their idols, do you ever find yourself retelling your community's 'sacred stories'? How can we best help people who have become over-reliant on their understanding of past glories and who are using these stories to avoid connecting with challenges of the present?

Responsibility
- Ezekiel challenges fatalism and blame-shifting. Where do we detect these attitudes today? Perhaps in talk of genetic programming, upbringing, global markets, karma or simply popular cynicism? Can we acknowledge that some of these factors are indeed significant in shaping people's lives, yet also insist that each generation must take responsibility? How shall we respond to people who say, 'God's not fair'?

- What about those whose desperation for security leads them to listen to the wrong voices? How can we best help them to make wise choices, while also letting them take responsibility for their decisions?

Leadership

- Ezekiel highlights some of the challenges and costs that can face those who are leaders and their churches and families. Pray for anyone who comes to mind.

- In addition to challenging those in leadership roles to show faithfulness and integrity, Ezekiel reminds us that Yahweh is a forgiving God of covenant commitment, who does not give up on his people in spite of their failings. How does that speak to your leaders, your church and yourself today?

Finally: Ezekiel is not an easy read. These two weeks working through the first half of the book might leave you with a sense of heavy going. If so, may I encourage you to persevere: there is good news according to Ezekiel, most of it still to come in the next issue of *Guidelines*. So please join us again after the (Christmas) break!

FURTHER READING

Leslie Allen, *Ezekiel 1–19* and *Ezekiel 20–48* (Word, 1990).

Walter Brueggemann, *Out of Babylon* (Abingdon Press, 2010).

Corrine L. Carvalho, *The Book of Ezekiel: Question by question* (Paulist Press, 2010).

John Goldingay, *Lamentations and Ezekiel for Everyone* (SPCK, 2016).

Paul M. Joyce, *Ezekiel: A commentary* (T&T Clark, 2007/09).

Christopher J.H. Wright, *The Message of Ezekiel* (IVP, 2001).

Luke 22:3—24:53

Steve Walton

Luke's gospel gathers pace as we read of Jesus' last days before his death and amazing resurrection. In these stories, disclosure takes place at several levels, and at each one Luke invites a response.

There is disclosure of *who Jesus truly is* – including to the highest court of Judaism. Jesus is Daniel's 'son of man', the mysterious figure vindicated by God, who is placed at God's right side in the place of executive authority in the universe. Jesus is God's son, the Messiah, as we have known since the divine voice declared this at his baptism and transfiguration (3:22; 9:35). Jesus is also one who serves and gives his life at great cost.

There is disclosure of *the meaning of Jesus' death*. At the last supper, Jesus explains his death using imagery from the Passover meal, which celebrates God's delivering his people from slavery in Egypt. Jesus reinterprets the bread and wine to speak of the deliverance he accomplishes through his coming death. Throughout the story of the cross, Luke stresses Jesus' innocence, and that he dies for guilty others. Multiple characters illustrate what the cross means and how to respond appropriately. The risen Jesus opens the disciples' minds to recognise him in all the Jewish scriptures, and thereby gives them a rich palette to paint the meaning of his life, death and resurrection.

There is disclosure of *what will come*, as the resurrection of Jesus opens the door into a new world. In this world, justice is seen, for Jesus has been vindicated by God's raising him from the dead. In this world, Jesus' resurrection body is the prototype of believers' resurrection bodies. This body is recognisably his yet sometimes is not recognised, can appear without warning in closed rooms and ascends to the Father's right side to share his authority. In this world, women's testimony is valid and welcome – the women play an 'apostolic' role as the messengers of the resurrection to the doubting male disciples.

As you read these chapters, look for these themes and see how they are expressed and developed. In many ways, the best commentary on this is Luke's book of Acts, as the transformed disciples proclaim the risen and ascended Jesus in the power of the promised Holy Spirit.

These notes make reference to both New Revised Standard Version (Anglicised) and the New International Version at different places, and you could use either as the basis of your reading of these chapters. Author references are to works in the 'Further Reading' list.

1 A 'both/and', not 'either/or', explanation

Luke 22:3–6

Satan returns to the story after being unmentioned for a while – we know from earlier in Luke that Jesus is here to battle against Satan/the devil and deliver people from his grasp (4:1–13; 8:12; 10:18; 11:18; 13:16). Now Satan's 'opportune time' (4:13) arrives and he seizes the chance to use Judas to forward his aims (v. 3).

Luke offers two levels of explanation concerning Judas' agreement to betray Jesus: a financial incentive (v. 5) and a spiritual takeover (v. 3). It would be easy to choose between these two and take only a naturalistic understanding – that it was the money which was important – or only an otherworldly understanding – that Judas was 'taken over' by Satan and had no choice. Luke paints a more complex picture: the two events of Satan 'entering' Judas and Judas going to the Jewish leaders are connected simply by 'and' (v. 4, NIV – the word is there in the original, although the NRSV does not translate it). No direct causal connection between the two events is stated.

As more widely in scripture, the way spiritual powers operate is in and through apparently 'human' events and choices. The cosmic, spiritual dimension is real, for sure – and Jesus' death will be the great deliverance from Satan for Israel and the world. And the human, mundane dimension is real too: Judas has genuine choice and himself makes the decision to go to the Jewish leaders (v. 4). Judas thus falls prey to the temptation of money, against which Jesus has frequently warned (e.g. 16:13–15), and fails to be alert so that he does not fall into temptation (21:34–36). Beyond this,

Luke – in common with the other gospels – does not let us inside Judas' mind to see his motives, and we are wise not to speculate.

The group who welcome Judas includes both the chief priests and the temple police (v. 4). Roman soldiers were not normally permitted into the temple courts, and the Roman rulers allowed the Jews to have their own security staff (we meet the captain of this staff in Acts 4:1). Their agreement with Judas is two-sided, entered into freely by both sides (v. 5), and leads to Judas looking for a chance to hand Jesus over to them (v. 6, NIV – NRSV has 'betray', although the word is more general than that suggests).

2 Passover prepared

Luke 22:7–13

The 14th day of the month of Nisan was the heart of the Passover celebration; on the afternoon of that day, the Passover lambs were slaughtered to recall the killing of the lambs at the exodus (Exodus 12:1–11). The blood of the exodus lambs was daubed on the Israelites' doorposts, so that the death of the firstborn would not afflict those homes (Exodus 12:12–13). In Jesus' day, Jewish people in Jerusalem celebrated Passover by eating lambs which had been killed in the temple courts on 14 Nisan, and then ate the lamb roasted that evening, which by Jewish reckoning was 15 Nisan (since the day began at sunset, 6.00 pm).

Jesus wanted to celebrate Passover with his disciples (v. 8), but was aware that the plot against him was growing. Jesus seems to have planned to hold his Passover meal a day before the official Passover, on the evening of 13 Nisan, in anticipation of his arrest. This would mean Jesus' death took place at the same time as the slaughter of the Passover lambs in the temple (see John 18:28; 19:14, which suggest that the trial of Jesus took place early on the morning of 14 Nisan and his death that afternoon).

As with Jesus' donkey ride (19:29–34), what looks like a pre-planned signal leads Peter and John to the right place. The man carrying a water jar (v. 10) would be unusual, since fetching water was normally the work of women or slaves. Jesus gives the two a coded formula to use, identifying himself as 'the Teacher' (v. 11) – a term never used in Luke by disciples when addressing Jesus.

'Passover' and 'prepare/preparation' are used four times each in this section, showing the focus on what is to follow – both Jesus' meal with his disciples and Jesus' death, to which the meal both points and explains. His death is a 'new Passover', just as his life and ministry is about bringing a 'new exodus' to the people of God. This time, the deliverance will be lasting, and it will go way beyond being freed from political oppression by freeing Israel and the world from the power of Satan and evil (see notes on 22:3).

3 Passover remixed

At Passover, a Jewish family eat reclining on couches around a low table (v. 14, NIV; NRSV is less precise). The couches and reclining posture mark this as a meal for free people, by contrast with the first Passover which was eaten standing, ready to leave Egypt (Exodus 12:11). Jesus' 'family' of disciples gather for the meal, which he identifies as a Passover (v. 15) – here is a hint of the new family which Jesus creates, the believing community (see the family language of 'brothers and sisters', e.g. Acts 1:16; 6:3, NIV).

This community will be created by Jesus, and specifically by the redeeming power of his death. Jesus' words and actions with the bread and wine enact and explain what is to come. Luke's account uniquely includes two of the four cups of wine drunk during the Passover supper (other accounts mention only one). Jesus relates the first cup to the coming kingdom (vv. 17–18), as he has done the whole meal (vv. 15–16) – God's rule will be seen through his coming death and resurrection.

Luke's phrasing of Jesus' actions with the bread, 'took… gave thanks… broke… gave' (v. 19) echoes the same sequence at the feeding of the five thousand (9:16) and with the two in Emmaus (24:30). The four actions were usual in a family meal, and Jesus takes them and refocuses them on his body, at that stage still present with them. His body is in the process of being given for them now, a process which will come to completion in his death. The form of the verb 'do [this]' (v. 19) indicates that they should *keep on* doing this action in future to remember what Jesus has done – his death is the most significant event in history, and his followers are to keep it front and centre in their hearts, minds and lives.

Jesus relates the second cup to his blood – his life laid down in death – as a new covenant (v. 20), a new agreement given by God to humanity. This covenant fulfils and replaces the exodus covenant given at Mount Sinai, which the Passover recalls for Jewish people. As believers drink from the cup in future, they will renew their grasp of the way Jesus has brought them into his family through his generous giving of himself.

4 Not to be served, but to serve

Luke 22:24–30

At the very point where Jesus is constituting the community as a new family of brothers and sisters, a dispute arises: who's the greatest (v. 24; see also 9:46–48)? Such arguments are common in human families and Jesus' new family will quickly be blighted by them if he does not act. Certainly, his family will need leadership after he departs; the crucial question is what kind of leadership is appropriate for the Jesus community.

Verses 25–30 are full of the language of power and authority: 'lord it', 'exercise authority', 'benefactors', 'greatest', 'leader/ruler', 'sit on thrones', 'judging'. These words all convey the way leaders of Jesus' day – and ours – operate, by dominating and imposing their will. Benefactors (v. 25) would have statues or inscriptions erected to celebrate their generosity to their city – such self-importance and boasting was considered appropriate in that time.

By contrast, Jesus wants those who lead his community to have an attitude of service (v. 26), focused on the needs of those they lead rather than on their own. Jesus himself models this (v. 27), and his forthcoming death is the epitome of true greatness. John portrays this powerfully in Jesus' washing his disciples' feet at this supper (John 13:1–17). Paul expresses the same theme in poetic form as Jesus leaving the glory of heaven, becoming human, 'taking the very nature of a servant', and following that path all the way to death on a cross (Philippians 2:5–8). Christian leadership is marked by the cross as the way to lead.

So, yes, the apostles will be given kingly rule over the twelve tribes of the renewed Israel that Jesus is forming (v. 30), but the kind of rule they exercise must be that of Jesus. His rule is given to him by his Father (v. 29) – the generous, gracious God who honours those who give themselves in a similarly generous and gracious way. The book of Acts shows how this plays out, as the apostles' teaching is central to the life of the new community (Acts 2:42; 4:19–20, 31, 33; 5:29–32, 42; 6:2, 7), and they are able to perform wonders and signs which also testify to God's generosity in Jesus (Acts 2:43; 3:6, 12–13, 16; 4:10; 5:12). Throughout, their focus is on exalting Jesus, not themselves.

5 Testing, testing (1)

Luke 22:31–38

When we are at our most vulnerable, we are frequently most tempted to sin. We may be tired, frightened or under pressure in one way or another – those are times when we need to be most aware of Satan's aim to undo our profession of faith in Jesus Christ and give in to his way of operating. Jesus knows this is the apostles' situation now (v. 31), and he prepares Simon in particular for what follows.

Jesus' words distinguish between the satanic testing which the whole apostle-group will face (v. 31) and his prayer for Simon Peter (v. 32). Peter is going to fall, but not ultimately fail, for Jesus has prayed for him. In spite of Peter's bold words (v. 33), Jesus warns that Peter will fall by denying that he knows Jesus (v. 34), but he promises that Peter will get up again and must then build up the faith of his fellows. Peter and Judas form an interesting pair (see 22:3–6), for they show that temptation and 'sifting' by Satan are not fatal: 'Satan can provoke a conflict, but he cannot determine its outcome' (Edwards, p. 638). The question is how a person responds to that testing; even a major failure, such as Peter's threefold denial of Jesus, does not have to be the end of the story. The book of Acts is again a powerful commentary on Jesus' words, as Peter takes a leading role in the Jesus family as spokesman and leader (Acts 1:15; 2:14; 3:1, 12; 4:8, 13, 19; 5:3, 8; 8:14; 9:32–35).

Jesus' next words point his disciples to their earlier mission of preparing for Jesus' visits to villages, when they relied on local hospitality (v. 35; 9:1–6). The situation is now different: the openness of people to Jesus during the mission in Galilee is being replaced by the rulers' hostility in Jerusalem, and the disciples must be ready (v. 36). The instruction to buy a sword is not intended literally, for Jesus' later words imply that he rejects carrying 'swords and clubs' (22:52). Nevertheless, some of the apostles take him literally (v. 38) and will mistakenly wield a sword at Jesus' arrest (22:49–50) – they still haven't understood that servant leadership means rejection of violence, and to that extent have succumbed to satanic testing already.

6 Testing, testing (2)

Luke 22:39–46

Further satanic testing afflicts the apostles and Jesus himself as his arrest approaches. The group go to their usual resting place, within an area where Passover pilgrims could stay (see 21:37; note 'as was his custom', v. 39, NRSV). This habit meant Judas could easily find them (22:47), and Jesus must have known that – nevertheless, he does not go elsewhere to avoid arrest, for he must fulfil God's purpose laid out in scripture (22:37). Jesus knows how hard the path he is following will be, and he not only prays himself but also asks his disciples to pray (v. 40). Luke paints the picture by sandwiching the disciples' (lack of) prayer (vv. 40, 45–46) around Jesus' agonising prayer (vv. 41–44), sharpening the contrast of the two events, which take place within a few metres of each other.

Jesus' prayer focuses on the 'cup' he will drink (v. 42). The prophets speak of God's judgement against sin as a cup which makes its drinkers helpless with drunkenness (e.g. Isaiah 51:17–23; Jeremiah 25:15–29). Thus Jesus' metaphor indicates that he will experience God's judgement – but vicariously, for he does not deserve it at all. That experience of judgement, and not the physical pain of the cross alone, is what horrifies Jesus and causes him to ask his Father that he might not have to go this way. Nevertheless, Jesus gets beyond his horror into a place of readiness to suffer if this is his Father's will: 'Not my will, but yours be done.' If verses 43–44 are original (they aren't in all our manuscripts of Luke), they portray God answering Jesus' prayer by strengthening him, and add to the sense of agony as Jesus anticipates his coming suffering.

The disciples, by contrast, are snoozing when they should be praying (v. 45). Luke does say that they sleep because of 'grief' (NRSV) or 'sorrow' (NIV) – their sadness at Jesus' words about his forthcoming arrest, trial and death saps their strength and they are exhausted. Jesus' response is to call them to imitate him, repeating his call to them to *keep* praying (the verb form in verses 40 and 46 suggests this) so that they are not victims to temptation – the way to meet temptation is to face it in prayer (compare 18:1).

Guidelines

The spiritual battle is reaching its peak as we approach the last day of Jesus' life. Satan is active in Judas (22:3) and is attacking the disciples (22:31).

Even Jesus is feeling the pressure as he looks down both barrels of the future (22:42, 44). Yet this is the most crucial phase of Jesus' life and ministry. Without his death on behalf of us sinners, his job will not be completed; he must carry through what scripture says about him (22:37). Our reaction to this must be great thankfulness at what Jesus does for us who live on this side of his death and resurrection. Because of his readiness and willingness to walk the journey all the way to the cross for us, we enjoy being members of his family, his new covenant people. This is why the supper of bread and wine can be called *eucharist*, for that word is derived from the Greek for 'give thanks' (used in 22:19).

How do you view the last supper? What response does it draw from you? If you belong to a church that uses a liturgy, look for the theme of thanksgiving for what Jesus does for us in the cross and resurrection in the service next time you attend. If your church doesn't use written liturgy, listen out for such thanksgiving in the prayers and music at the supper. If you help in leading your church's worship, whether in word or music, reflect on how you can enable your congregation to engage thankfully with God in the supper.

Jesus' example of prayer when facing the agony of his path to the cross invites us to be prayerful in the face of pressure (22:41–44). It's all too easy when the going gets tough to give up; Jesus calls us to pray and keep praying (22:40, 46). That's not to say it's easy, but two things will strengthen us: knowing that Jesus is praying too (22:32, 41–44; compare Hebrews 7:25; Romans 8:34); and praying with others, as the disciples could have done (22:40, 46 – the instruction in both cases is to the whole group). Whatever form your church's corporate prayer life takes, this section of Luke asks you how you can be involved in that.

1 The hour of darkness

Luke 22:47–53

Under cover of darkness, the forces of darkness make their move, led by Judas (v. 47). A kiss would normally be the affectionate greeting of a loyal friend, but when Judas kisses Jesus, it identifies the one the crowd have come to take – for in the dark garden, they might not be able to recognise

Jesus (v. 48). Judas' disloyalty and betrayal are complete, and we hear nothing more of him until the story of his tragic death (Acts 1:16–19).

It is not only Judas who betrays what Jesus is about: Jesus' other disciples seek to defend him by violence (vv. 49–50). They don't understand Jesus' rejection of military might as a way of operating, which goes all the way back to Jesus' refusal of Satan's offer of the kingdoms of the world (4:5–8). At this time, they fail to grasp that Jesus' way of living and dying is to give himself into the hands of God's purposes, rather than carrying weapons (22:37–38).

Jesus' next actions show, by contrast, what his way looks like. He heals the ear of the high priest's servant, showing love for enemies even when they mistreat him (v. 51, see 6:27). By juxtaposing their swords and clubs, and the darkness in which they come, with his open teaching in the temple (vv. 52–53), Jesus shows his enemies what a huge act of injustice they are performing. He is not a 'bandit' (v. 52, NRSV). This word is later used for the armed Zealots who rebelled against the Romans in the mid-60s AD, and that later knowledge is probably behind the NIV's (somewhat anachronistic) 'leading a rebellion'. At this period, 'bandit' has a wider sense of robbers and thieves who beat up travellers and stole from them (such as in the parable of the good Samaritan; see 10:30). Jesus' way is not thuggery and violence, creeping around in the dark to get what he wants; rather, he speaks in the open and lets people judge what to do with his teaching and claims.

The contrast of darkness and light here underlines the sense of Satan's assault on Jesus and his people: 'this is… the power of darkness' (v. 53) – and things are going to get darker still.

2 The trial of Peter

Luke 22:54–62

The night-time events continue as Jesus is bundled off to the high priest's house, followed by Peter (v. 54). The nights can be cold at Passover time (March/April) in Jerusalem, and the fire would keep those waiting warm. Those who speak to Peter may well include some of the arrest party, since they recognise him (vv. 56, 58). The third one recognises Peter's northern (Galilean) accent (v. 59). Sitting in the courtyard, they could see into the house proper where Jesus was speaking with the high priest.

This point in Jesus' trial (vv. 54; 22:63–65) is a preliminary hearing which leads to the formal hearing before the Sanhedrin the next morning (22:66). It corresponds to Matthew's and Mark's accounts of the first part of Jesus' trial (Matthew 26:57–68; Mark 14:53–65). The preliminary and formal hearings would inevitably overlap considerably in the ground they covered: the first, more informal hearing established the facts of the case and identified the charge that should be brought, and the second, more formal hearing decided on action to be taken.

Peter himself is as truly on trial as Jesus through the questions put to him, and these events fulfil Jesus' warning that before morning (the cock crow) Peter would three times deny that he knows Jesus (22:34). Luke (and other gospels) do not say what was going on in Peter's mind during this event – in common with other ancient writers, they do not psychologise their characters – but we can recognise the danger Peter would have faced if he had admitted to knowing Jesus. The standard way to deal with rebels was to kill the leader and then his followers would give up and disappear (see Acts 5:36–37), and Peter faced such a danger here, especially if he were recognised as Jesus' number two and thus the next leader in line.

With one look from Jesus, Peter recognises what he has done (v. 61) and he is heartbroken (v. 62). His weeping speaks of his 'turning back', promised by Jesus (22:32), and marks Peter as beginning the road which will take him to leadership in Jesus' community after Pentecost. Failure is not final with Jesus – there is a way back.

3 The trial of Jesus

Luke 22:63–71

Luke tells of Peter's and Jesus' trials back-to-back, highlighting similarities and contrasts, although the two events went on simultaneously in adjacent spaces, for Jesus could see Peter (22:61).

The first event is a preliminary hearing (vv. 63–65). It was standard practice to gain information by violence (see Acts 22:24), and physical attacks on Jesus were reinforced by mockery and insults. These Jewish guards assume the messiah would be able to identify an attacker without seeing them, apparently based on Isaiah 11:3, 'He shall not judge by what his eyes see.' The irony is that what they say about Jesus being a prophet is true, for Jesus accurately predicted both Peter's denial and the abuse he himself now faces (22:34; 18:31–32).

The second event is a formal hearing before the Sanhedrin, the supreme Jewish council. Caiaphas, as high priest, would chair the meeting (he is named as high priest in 3:2), and it probably took place in the council chamber within the temple precincts. Capital trials, according to later Jewish laws, could not take place at night, and so it is daytime (v. 66).

By contrast with Peter, Jesus tells the truth. The crucial issue is his identity: is he the Messiah (v. 67)? Jesus' answer initially appears evasive, but he then identifies himself using his favourite designation 'the son of man' (v. 69), which the Sanhedrin would know he used regularly. He identifies himself as the one taken to God, vindicated and given universal rule (see Daniel 7:13–14 – NRSV translates 'a human being' rather than NIV's 'a son of man'). Jesus places himself alongside Israel's God and claims that he will reign with God. The Sanhedrin's next question to Jesus is if he is 'the son of God', which is a messianic title, and Jesus' answer, 'You say that I am' (v. 70), is positive enough for them to come to a verdict (v. 71). Jesus' response is probably saying, 'Yes, but I might not be using the words as you are.'

Jesus' identity is now fully disclosed: his reign at God's right side in heaven is coming, rather than his being a political or military messiah. Jesus was identified as 'the son of God' by God's voice (3:22; 9:35) and by demons (4:3, 9, 41; 8:28), and he now connects that to being 'the son of man', the powerful ruler of all (9:26; 12:8).

4 The innocent Jesus, Pilate and Herod

Luke 23:1–12

The four gospels each offer their own portrait of the climactic event of Jesus' death. As we listen to Luke's telling, we shall hear a strong emphasis on Jesus as the innocent one who dies for his guilty people. Each section of Luke 23 portrays this theme, and different characters offer different angles on it. In this part, we encounter Jesus' innocence through the manifestly false charges of the Sanhedrin (vv. 1–2) and through Pilate's and Herod's responses (vv. 3–12).

The Sanhedrin brought Jesus to Pilate, the Roman governor, claiming three charges (v. 2), and careful readers of Luke know that all three were untrue. Jesus was not subverting the nation; rather, the Sanhedrin were, by acting complicitly with the Romans and failing to stand out as God's holy people. Jesus did not forbid paying taxes to Caesar; rather, he relativised

Caesar's power as less than that of God (20:21–26). Ironically, the Sanhedrin participated in collecting taxes for Rome. And Jesus was not claiming to be an earthly king, the charge which the Sanhedrin hoped would stick with the Roman governor; rather, he said his kingly rule will be exercised at God's right side (22:69). The Sanhedrin, in collaborating with the Romans, were denying God's ultimate rule. All these charges were true of Israel and her leaders, but not of Jesus – and he will die as a consequence.

Pilate makes a series of tactical errors in dealing with the situation. He is known for earlier rushing to unwise action against the Jewish people, and here his readiness to act politically rather than justly comes through: his primary concern is to keep the Sanhedrin onside. His first error is to declare Jesus innocent more than once – in fact, three times in total (vv. 4, 14, 22) – rather than simply saying it once and that being the end of the matter.

Pilate's second error is to try to fob the Sanhedrin off by sending Jesus to Herod, who is a superficial man, wanting to see a sign (v. 8). When Herod doesn't get what he wants, he reacts like a spoiled child, mocking Jesus (v. 11). Herod is a man whose greatest interest is himself: he wants a conjuror, not a messiah; entertainment, rather than thinking about his standing with God.

5 The innocent Jesus and the guilty Barabbas

Luke 23:13–25

Pilate continues down the slippery slope to complicity in Jesus' murder. Even having Herod's verdict of innocent (but not entertaining), he slides further – he concedes that Jesus does not deserve death, but proposes to flog him (vv. 13–16). This is unjust, for Pilate and Herod believe Jesus to be innocent, but it reflects Pilate's desire to keep the Jewish leaders happy.

Pilate has a further chance to free Jesus, for there is a Roman custom to free one prisoner at Passovers which lies behind the crowd's call to release Barabbas (v. 18). The other gospels explicitly describe this custom (Matthew 27:15; Mark 15:6; John 18:39); a scribe inserted it into a manuscript of Luke as verse 17 (missing in English versions, since translators recognise it as not original). The rent-a-mob that the Sanhedrin assembled early on this Passover morning cry out for this known criminal to be released – we should not mistake this for the same group as the Passover pilgrims who greeted Jesus (19:37–40) and thus think of them as fickle. This was a carefully planned plot to get rid of Jesus.

Pilate repeats for a third time that Jesus is not guilty (v. 22) as the crowd cries for his blood (vv. 21, 23). The initiative for Jesus' death comes from the Jewish leaders, not the Romans – and that would be of significance in Luke's commending the gospel message to Romans. It is also clear that Pilate is weak, as he has now slid to the bottom of the slippery slope: he passes sentence against Jesus and frees the guilty Barabbas (v. 25).

Luke strikingly juxtaposes Barabbas' guilt (v. 19) and Jesus' innocence – the 'exchange' of the innocent Jesus and the guilty Barabbas portrays clearly the way in which Jesus dies for and on behalf of many more guilty people. Imagine the story from Barabbas' perspective: he knows he is to be executed, and yet the soldiers fetch him and tell him that he is free. When he asks (as he surely must have done) why he is being freed, he is told that another will be crucified instead: Jesus. The name 'Barabbas' means 'son of the father': the Father's true Son, Jesus, dies in places of one bearing his name.

6 How to respond to the innocent, dying Jesus

Luke 23:26–43

The theme of Jesus' innocence runs on through this section. Jesus is the 'green tree', full of life, an innocent man, and he dies rather than the 'dry tree' of Israel, which deserves death (v. 31). Characters around the cross show how to respond to Jesus' innocent death.

Simon of Cyrene gets only a brief mention (v. 26), but is significant. When a condemned criminal was taken out for execution, he would be surrounded by four Roman soldiers, with a fifth walking in front carrying a placard bearing the charge against him. For Jesus, this read, 'This is the king of the Jews' (v. 38). The procession took the long way to the place of execution, so that people would see and be warned. The prisoner carried the crossbeam – the whole cross would be too heavy to bear. However, Jesus was too weak even for this, and so Simon felt the tap of a Roman spear on his shoulder, meaning that he must serve the Romans by carrying Jesus' crossbeam. Mark's naming Simon's sons (Mark 15:21 – Rufus may also be the one named in Romans 16:13) may suggest that Simon became a believer. Simon models 'carrying the cross', which Jesus identifies as a characteristic of his followers (9:23; 14:27). Paul picks this image up in writing of his desire to participate in Jesus' sufferings, 'becoming like him in his death' (Philippians 3:10–11).

The two thieves portray wrong and right responses. One rails against Jesus: like Herod, he wants proof, a messiah who will save him from death and come down from the cross (v. 39). The other acknowledges the truth of Jesus' innocence and his own guilt (v. 41). In a flash of insight, he asks Jesus not to save him *from* death, but to save him *through* death (v. 42). He understands that Jesus will be a king and asks for his remembrance, and gets far more than he expects: Jesus promises that he will be in paradise *today* (v. 43). 'Paradise' comes from a word meaning 'garden', and conjures up thoughts of freedom, comfort and joy – humanity's story began in a garden (Genesis 2:8–9, 15). Jesus' death now offers that liberty to Luke's readers as they, like the second thief, recognise their guilt and seek Jesus' aid.

Guidelines

It's easy to focus on how much Jesus suffers as we read the story of the cross. It's interesting, therefore, that none of the New Testament writers pay much attention to the extent of Jesus' suffering. Their focus is on the meaning of his death, and each gospel offers different angles on that meaning, enriching our understanding as we consider the four.

Luke's focus on Jesus' innocence, and correspondingly our guilt, invites us to reflect on Jesus' offer of forgiveness. We can superficially gloss over our sins on the basis that 'God will forgive; that's his job' (Heinrich Heine), and forget that forgiveness requires our repentance. Like the second thief, we need to admit our guilt and ask Jesus to welcome us; only then do we hear Jesus' promise of being with him in paradise. This truth calls us to recognise when we sin and then turn back to God speedily to seek forgiveness.

Earlier generations of Christians practised self-examination on a regular basis, spending time regularly – often daily – identifying areas where they were failing to be the people God called them to be. 'Sin' has become an unpopular theme in the world and sometimes in church: people prefer to be told what they're good at and what potential they have, rather than to have their failings highlighted. Consider where you sin, particularly 'besetting' sins which catch you out often, and be sure to 'keep short accounts' with God – turning back to him as soon as you are aware that you have failed. Then you will continue to live in the experience of Jesus' forgiving love.

It's not that Christians are to be negative, gloomy people – Luke ends his story with rejoicing and praising God (24:52–53). However, joy comes as we recognise and turn from our sin to Jesus; the forgiven life is a joyful life! When we invite others to engage with Jesus, we are inviting them first to recognise that they are less than God intends. We cannot, in truth, simply tell people that God loves them and so all will be well; the pathway to their experience of God's love is through the cross of Jesus, as they bring their sins, lay them at the foot of the cross and walk on forgiven.

1 The innocent Jesus dies

Luke 23:44–53

Nature participates in the action as Jesus hangs between earth and heaven on the cross. The sun is darkened (vv. 44–45a); so awful is this time when Jesus bears the world's sin that nature turns its back. Passover occurs at the full moon, so this could not be a solar eclipse; Luke is portraying a remarkable otherworldly event. Darkness in scripture symbolises God's absence (recall the night of Jesus' arrest, 22:53), and thus pictures God's anger and pain at the injustice done to Jesus (see also Amos 8:9–10).

The temple, whose veil was torn (v. 45b), was divided into sections, with growing limitations as to who could enter as you went further in. A large, heavy curtain sealed off the holy of holies, where only the high priest went once a year, on the day of atonement. The holy of holies was the space where God was considered present – and thus it was a dangerous place. When the high priest entered, he had bells on his robe so that those outside could hear that he was still moving and had not been killed by God! This curtain's tearing means the danger of God's holiness is gone – God is not confined in this space in order to keep people safe, but is in the world, accessible, through the death of Jesus. The book of Acts provides eloquent commentary on this, as people encounter God through Jesus and by the Spirit in many places and cities.

Jesus' job is now done, and he gives himself into his Father's hands, echoing Psalm 31:5 (v. 46). These words express trust and confidence. His 'spirit' is not a particular part of him – that would be to think in Greek, rather than biblical, ways about people. Rather, Jesus expires, 'breathes his last', as we say.

Two responses to Jesus' death underline Jesus' innocence at the end of the story. The Roman centurion – a Gentile – recognises what Jesus has done by declaring him innocent (v. 47). Joseph of Arimathea is a dissident member of the Sanhedrin, a secret Jesus-follower (vv. 50–51b), and gives Jesus a dignified burial in a tomb cut in rock. This is not a criminal's burial – such men were normally thrown into a large common grave – but that of a man who is honoured.

2 Women witness the empty tomb and learn its meaning

Luke 23:54—24:12

Female followers of Jesus are prominent in Luke. They travel with and provide for Jesus and his disciples (8:1–3). Martha and Mary give hospitality (10:38–42). Jesus delivers a woman bent over by a spirit (13:10–17), and heals a woman suffering from excessive menstrual bleeding (8:43–48). Here, it is women who prepare to take care of Jesus' body by gathering sweet-smelling spices and perfumes, a traditional way of covering the smell of a decomposing body in a warm climate (23:56a). However, Jesus' death at about 3.00 pm (23:44) made it impossible to complete all that was required before the sabbath began at 6.00 pm, and so the women could do no more until Sunday (23:56b). They took careful note of the tomb's location (23:55) – a signal to Luke's readers that they did not mistakenly go to the wrong tomb 36 hours later.

Early Sunday morning, there were the women, ready to honour the body of Jesus (24:1). The round stone, sitting in a slot in the rock just in front of the tomb, had been rolled away, to their surprise – although it would enable them to get to the body more easily (24:2). A bigger surprise was that the body was not there (24:3), and an even bigger surprise was the message from the angels (divine messengers dressed in white) that Jesus was risen from the dead (24:4–5). The angels then reminded these Galilean women of what he had said in their region (24:6): what the angels say (24:7) summarises Jesus' words in 9:22, 44; 18:33.

Luke's reporting has a strong claim to be historical, for no Jew would invent a story where the primary witnesses were women, especially to a unique event like this. The disciples' reaction to the women's story shows the scepticism Jewish men had about women's words (24:11). Luke not only says they are women, but names three of them: Mary Magdalene and

Joanna were in the travelling group (8:2–3), and 'Mary the mother of James' is most likely the mother of one of the Jameses among the twelve (6:14–15). The naming of these individuals probably indicates that they are the source of this story – that's how eyewitnesses were identified in ancient writing.

3 Clarifying the picture (1)

Luke 24:13–24

Luke records two main appearances of the risen Jesus. Like the other gospel writers, Luke is selective in the resurrection stories he tells.

This first story introduces us to two disciples from Judea – Emmaus may have been their home (v. 13). Cleopas is otherwise unknown, and his unnamed companion may have been his wife. They could have been Passover pilgrims, present for recent events (vv. 18–21), including the earlier part of the day when they heard the women's report (vv. 22–23).

Jesus begins walking and talking with them and they are 'kept from recognising him' (v. 16, NIV), rather as the meaning of Jesus' words had been hidden from his disciples (9:45; 18:34). This passive verb suggests that God is the one who prevents them recognising Jesus at this point – for God has plans that require them listening to Jesus for a while. These disciples are being given the 'more' of the 'secrets of the kingdom' which Jesus has promised to them (8:10, 18) – including the nature of his resurrection – and so they need to listen carefully and absorb what Jesus says. The resurrection body of Jesus evidently does not appear 'otherworldly', but as that of a human like other humans.

Cleopas and his companion describe the debate about Jesus in summary form: it was widely agreed that he was a prophet (v. 19, see 4:24; 7:16; 9:8, 19; 13:33), and his followers' hope was that he was the Messiah, 'the one to redeem Israel' (v. 21). But they expressed their hope in a past tense: 'we *had* hoped' (v. 21) – their hope had been disappointed. They do not expect that Jesus will rise from the dead, even though he spoke about it (9:22; 18:33) and the angel's message told them about it (24:7). These are not people psychologically open to visions of a dead friend, but people in deep disappointment.

As well as their disappointment, they are puzzled by the women's report (vv. 22–23), which others have checked (v. 24). 24:12 records only Peter visiting the tomb, but this plural group, 'some of those who were with us' (NRSV), fits well with John's account, where Peter and John are the first male disciples to visit the tomb (John 20:3–10).

This part of the Emmaus walk story lays out the questions well: what's going on? Who was Jesus? What do the women's words mean? Cleopas and his companion need their eyes to be opened, and that's what will happen next.

4 Clarifying the picture (2)

Luke 24:25–32

So far post-resurrection, Jesus has only asked a question (24:17). Now he responds to Cleopas and his companion's questions in two ways that would have looked familiar to Luke's Christian readers: by word and sacrament.

First, Jesus gives a biblical seminar in which he shows them who he is and what he has come to do (vv. 25–27). Jesus reshapes their understanding of what kind of messiah he is through the lens of the scriptures. He is a Messiah who had to suffer before gaining power and glory, by contrast with many Jewish expectations that the messiah would be a military leader who would free the Jews from Roman subjugation. Rather than causing others to suffer, Jesus as Messiah suffered himself, as he had said scripture foretold (18:33). Luke names two of the major parts of the Jewish canon of scripture, the books of Moses (Genesis to Deuteronomy) and the prophets (the historical books and the prophetic books), and then writes 'all the scriptures' (v. 27) – these are the resources for understanding Jesus. That is why early Christian preaching and teaching was rooted in seeing Jesus this way, as the true subject of scripture. The book of Acts and the New Testament letters are stuffed with echoes of scripture, as the authors mine its testimony to Jesus, and they do so because Jesus himself did it first.

Second, Jesus breaks bread with them (vv. 30–32). It would be good Jewish practice to offer hospitality to strangers, and Cleopas and his companion insist that he should stay the night (vv. 28–29) – it would not be safe to travel alone when bandits and robbers could attack under cover of darkness. Then two surprises happen. First, Jesus takes the role of the host at the meal, rather than a guest, by blessing God for the food they have. Second, Jesus repeats his actions from the last supper and from the feeding of the five thousand: he takes bread, gives thanks, breaks it and gives it to them (v. 30; see 9:16; 22:19). This fourfold action at the feeding was probably Jesus' regular practice, his adaptation of Jewish practice at mealtimes. And this opens their eyes to recognise Jesus himself and their experience on the road with him (vv. 31–32).

5 Clarifying the picture (3)

Luke 24:33–43

The Emmaus two immediately return to Jerusalem (v. 33) – this news is too good not to share! Their experience of meeting Jesus is confirmed by his appearing to Simon too (v. 34), an appearance only otherwise mentioned by Paul (1 Corinthians 15:5). They know for sure that Jesus is risen from the dead, but what kind of life does he now have? What kind of person is he? The next few moments answer those questions.

The verb form of 'stood' (v. 36) suggests that Jesus appears abruptly and suddenly among the disciples, and that explains their terrified response, thinking that he is a ghost (v. 37). They do not yet understand that Jesus is risen, and so they see his appearance through superstitious eyes. Jewish people of the time expected the resurrection of the dead – a physical resurrection – at the end of the age (Daniel 12:2–3). But they are not expecting one man to be raised from the dead and then for history to continue – hence their shock when this happens to Jesus.

Jesus reassures them by inviting them to touch him, showing them his hands and feet, and by eating (vv. 39–43). The hands and feet still have the marks of Jesus' wounds from the cross, according to John 20:25, and thus they would be sure not only that he was physically raised, but also that it truly was Jesus. Eating shows that he is not a visitor from Sheol, the mysterious abode of the dead where people lived a ghostly existence (see also Acts 1:4; 10:41; John 21:10–15).

Luke sharpens our understanding of Jesus' resurrection further in this story. Jesus is, as Paul will say, the first fruits of the resurrection (1 Corinthians 15:20, 23), the first to experience this transformation that God accomplishes into a new kind of life. This new life is physical, but more than physical: after his resurrection, Jesus can suddenly appear and go unrecognised, and yet also has the marks of his suffering. The disciples, Luke stresses, are not having a vision or dream – ancient people knew as well as modern people what those were. Rather, they are experiencing Jesus as the prototype of what they will become in the world to come.

6 Transition and mission

Jesus prepares his disciples for the days ahead in two ways. First, he enlarges their understanding, as he did with the Emmaus pair (vv. 44–46). Second, he tells them the task they will fulfil and promises them power to carry it out (vv. 47–49).

The disciples' understanding of Jesus through the lens of the scriptures is going to be very important, for that understanding will enable them to explain the significance of Jesus to their fellow Jews. The mention of 'the law of Moses, the prophets and the psalms' (v. 44) names the three parts of the Hebrew canon of scripture: the Pentateuch (Genesis to Deuteronomy), the prophets (the historical books and the prophets) and the writings (of which Psalms is the first book). This, incidentally, shows that the Hebrew Bible was probably complete in Jesus' day.

Jesus treats the whole Bible as speaking about him, and then outlines the key threads to look for in reading what we know as the Old Testament (vv. 46–47). The Messiah will suffer – itself a new interpretation of scripture, for there is no evidence of a suffering messiah prior to Jesus. The Messiah will rise from the dead on the third day. These two Jesus has fulfilled. The latter two points then look to the future: by Jesus' authority ('in his name') people will hear the message of forgiveness through repentance; and this message will go to all peoples, not just the Jews, although it will begin in the Jewish capital, Jerusalem. The book of Acts shows how this takes place.

Jesus then makes a key pair of promises to the disciples: they will give testimony to the events of his life, ministry, death and resurrection (v. 48), and he will empower them for the task by sending his Father's promise (v. 49). 'The Father's promise' refers to the Spirit, who will come at Pentecost (Acts 2); the Acts accounts of Jesus' ascension and Peter's sermon make this meaning clear (Acts 1:4, 8; 2:33). The disciples will bear witness to the saving events of Jesus' death and resurrection – but they are not left to do this alone; the Spirit's power will enable them to do what they could not otherwise do.

Guidelines

The resurrection of Jesus is the central event of history, for through it the new age has invaded our age; because of it, the power of the Holy Spirit is available to humans who trust in Christ; because of it, we are confident of our own resurrection and that of others who trust in Christ, in due time. It is a revolutionary happening!

The resurrection of Jesus is also one of the most puzzling events in history, for it is outside our experience. We know, as the ancients did, that dead people do not rise. We recognise that when people say they've been seeing dead relatives again – as quite a number do – that they are projecting their desires outwards, rather than experiencing something objectively real.

Yet the evidence for this remarkable event is solid and persuasive. The change in the disciples is stunning: they went from fear and lack of expectation – they even thought that Jesus was a ghost (24:37) – to confidence and readiness to speak of Jesus (Acts 2). Some claim that the disciples stole and hid Jesus' body and then said that he was risen; but their willingness to suffer for their claims would be amazing if they had stolen the body – people do not lay down their lives for a lie. The Jewish authorities only had to produce the body if the tomb was not empty. The appearances of Jesus, to different people at different times and in different places, do not have the classic marks of hallucinations or visions. The resurrection of Jesus is the best explanation of this evidence.

To think more about the evidence for Jesus' resurrection, read one of the classic studies, such as Gary R. Habermas and Michael R. Licona, *The Case for the Resurrection of Jesus* (Kregel, 2004) or Frank Morison, *Who Moved the Stone?* (Faber and Faber, 1962). Morison, a journalist, takes readers on his journey of considering the evidence and being persuaded by it. Habermas and Licona aim to explain the case to equip Christians to speak to others about the resurrection of Jesus. Try explaining the resurrection to a Christian friend to see how good your grasp of it is, so that you can grow in confidence in explaining your faith to others.

FURTHER READING

James R. Edwards, *The Gospel according to Luke (Pillar New Testament Commentary)* (Eerdmans, 2015) – a meatier commentary for those who want to dig deeper.

R.T. France, *Luke (Teach the Text)* (Baker, 2013) – a wonderful commentary with good explanations of the text and helpful ideas for preaching and teaching.

Tom Wright, *Luke for Everyone* (SPCK, 2001) – clear, thoughtful devotional reading of the whole gospel.

Proverbs 1—29

Ernest Lucas

Proverbs is about wisdom (1:2). In the Old Testament, wisdom can be defined as 'the ability to cope with life in the best possible way'. The topics covered in Proverbs show this: for example, family, friends, neighbours, poverty and wealth, agriculture, commerce, law courts and the royal court.

Today, people advertise services as 'life coaches' to mentor people in 'life skills'. In education, social work and industry, emphasis is put on the importance of mentoring. The mentors in Proverbs are parents (1:8; 6:20), primarily the father. The child addressed is the son. The NRSV uses the word 'child', but the Hebrew and context make clear that this is a son. This gender bias upsets some readers. This problem is not unique to Proverbs. God's revelation has always taken an 'enfleshed' form, especially in Jesus (John 1:18). It is always 'clothed' in a particular historical and cultural situation. When applying any part of the Bible to our life today, we have to carry out 'cultural transposition'. First, we imagine ourselves in the position of the original addressee(s) in order to understand what the message was for them. We then must consider prayerfully and imaginatively how it might apply to ourselves today, in a different historical and cultural setting, whether we are women or men.

In our first week, we will study Proverbs 1—9. This consists of several carefully constructed 'lessons' in which a father is mentoring his son, who seems to be on the point of launching out to life in the big wide world. In the second week, we will study some of the themes that run through Proverbs 10—29. In a later study, we will look at some of the 'characters' in Proverbs and the different types of literature it contains.

Unless otherwise stated, Bible quotations are from the New Revised Standard Version (Anglicised).

1 Proverbs' purpose and wisdom's appeal

Proverbs 1:1–7, 20–33

Proverbs is attributed to Solomon as the founder of the tradition of wisdom teaching in Israel. A series of subheadings (22:17; 24:23; 25:1; 30:1; 31:1) and changes in form and style indicate that the book contains material from various sources and times, but it has a unified purpose: to impart wisdom (vv. 2–7). Three things are said about wisdom: it has cognitive content and can be learned by study and application (vv. 2, 5); it has practical application in how we live (vv. 3a, 4); and, significantly, sandwiched in the middle of this (v. 3b), it has a moral basis. In the Old Testament, 'righteousness' refers to a right moral order in society, 'justice' is the moral quality which maintains this order in being and 'equity' means treating everyone fairly. This morality has a spiritual root: 'the fear of the Lord' (v. 7). As Proverbs 8:13a says, 'The fear of the Lord is hatred of evil.' Put simply, the fear of the Lord is loyalty and love for God that is shown in obedience to God's commands.

Proverbs offers wisdom to the 'simple', those who are inexperienced and untaught and so might easily be led astray. This is likely to be true of the young, who therefore should heed parental teaching. However, there are depths in the book from which the mature, the wise, can learn. A Hebrew proverb can be described as 'a realistic observation on life crystallised in a brief memorable sentence'. Because of their brevity, they can be enigmatic, and wisdom is needed to appreciate their meaning and application.

Among the lessons there are some interludes. In the first (vv. 20–33), wisdom is personified as a woman offering wisdom to everyone in a prophet-like way. This makes clear the availability of wisdom for all who want it. She gives dire warnings of disaster to those who are too morally perverse ('fools') or too arrogant ('scoffers') to seek wisdom and who lead the simple astray. Those who heed her will find security in life. Strikingly, she says and claims things which elsewhere are only said or claimed by God, such as pouring out her 'spirit' (v. 23, 'thoughts' in the NRSV; see Joel 2:28) and hiding from the wicked when they seek her (v. 28; see Hosea 5:6). Wisdom stands close to God and shares divine authority.

2 Money and power

Money, power and sex are often said to be the major motives for doing evil. In his first lesson, the father deals with money and power.

Intrinsic to the lessons is the 'instruction' form of wisdom saying. This consists of a command followed by a motive for obeying it. Sometimes conditions are added. This lesson begins with a general command and motive, followed by a condition (vv. 8–10a). There is then another command followed by a more specific condition (vv. 10b–14). It ends with the main command and motive (vv. 15–19).

The sinners' words (vv. 11–14) offer the exercising of power over 'the innocent'. 'Sheol' is the Hebrew word for the abode of the dead, but it is was also seen as a power that invades and weakens life. Here, it is personified as a fearsome monster. The sinners hold out the prospect of wielding such power, which will lead to great material rewards (v. 13). A get-rich-quick scheme is dangled before the son. There is an element of peer pressure involved in the temptation – become one of the gang and share a common lot and purse (v. 14). The young may be particularly prone to yield to such pressure. However, older people are affected by it too, from the desire to 'keep up with the Joneses' to the pressure to submit to the corporate culture of a work situation. Christians face constant pressure to conform to the values of our culture, rather than to stand out as salt and light (Matthew 5:13–16). Conforming uncritically to a particular church culture can be harmful to spiritual growth.

The father supports his main command by two motives. The first (v. 16) is a simple declaration that the sinners' behaviour is wrong. This is an appeal to the youth's conscience. We should never discount this appeal to 'natural law ethics' in our dialogue with people. All humans are made in the image of God, and even in our fallen state there is some sense of right and wrong. Second, he brands their behaviour as stupid because it will eventually lead to disaster (vv. 17–19) – an appeal to 'consequential ethics'.

This lesson is a cartoon-like picture of a murderous mugging, but it can be transposed into behaviour in everyday situations in the family, at work or in the community.

3 Trust in the Lord

The start of this lesson promises the son long life and 'abundant welfare' (v. 2) if he follows his father's teaching. The Hebrew word translated as 'abundant welfare' is *shalom*. Its basic meaning is indicated in Numbers 6:24–26, where it is translated as 'peace'. It sums up the well-being which flows from living in a right relationship to God and enjoying God's blessings. The father then makes the point that the kind of person you are is more important than what you earn or own (vv. 3–4). This, in turn, is rooted in your relationship with God, which should be marked by four things: trust in the Lord, acknowledging him, the fear of the Lord and honouring the Lord with the material goods with which you are blessed (vv. 5–10).

In the context of Proverbs, and what has been said in verses 3–4, the promise of 'straight paths' is as much, if not more, a promise of living a morally good life as of material success. In the context of the rhetoric of motivation, the language of verses 8 and 10 should be taken as hyperbole, depicting a paradisiacal situation. Any attempt to base a 'health-and-wealth' gospel on them is dispelled by verses 11–12. These do not promise an easy life, but one of discipline. Discipline can take two forms: corrective discipline, which is applied to wrong behaviour; and formative discipline, which is not related to doing wrong but is needed to develop good qualities and skills. This can be painful, as athletes, musicians and craft-workers know.

The interlude which follows praises wisdom, again personified as a woman (vv. 13–20). She is said to be of more value, and a better investment, than material wealth – another indication that the language of verse 10 is not to be taken too literally. Having wisdom is the true basis for life (v. 18). Mention of the 'tree of life', with its echo of the creation story, prepares the way for what is said in verses 19–20. Wisdom can offer the benefits she does because the Lord created the world by wisdom. Therefore, those who live by wisdom do so in accordance with the fundamental structure and purpose of the created order, and so will enjoy *shalom*.

4 The two ways

In the first (vv. 1–9) of three lessons contained in this chapter, the father begins by reminiscing about his own education and quoting some of his father's teaching. This builds a bond of empathy with his sons – he has been in their position. It also presents himself as a model of what he is exhorting them to do: pay attention to parental teaching. In addition, it gives his teaching authority because it has been tried and tested down the generations by experience. The body of the lesson is an exhortation to value and get wisdom. The NIV 1984 translation conveys the sense of verse 7 well: 'Wisdom is supreme; therefore get wisdom. Though it cost all you have, get understanding.'

The second lesson (vv. 10–19) sets out starkly the metaphor of 'the two ways' which pervades Proverbs. The way of wisdom, 'the paths of uprightness', is described in verses 11–13. The father's teaching has already set his son on it (v. 11), and he is urged to stay on it by following the instruction of wisdom. It is a safe path, free of obstruction (v. 12). 'The path of the wicked' is described vividly in verses 14–17, though it is those on it who are described – a cast of abhorrent characters. The repeated admonitions against joining them imply that the choice of path is something that has to be made quite often. It is as if at times the path of the wicked comes close enough to the right path to provide a tempting alternative and an active choice has to be made to avoid it. The closing verses use light/dark imagery in a striking way. The imagery of verse 18 implies that gaining wisdom is a dynamic process of growth.

The third lesson (vv. 20–27) stresses the importance of vigilance in order to remain on the right path. Paul urges his readers, 'No longer present your members to sin as instruments of wickedness' (Romans 6:13). The father's words here provide a commentary on this as he refers to the right use of bodily members.

Jesus' exhortation to enter the narrow gate and follow the narrow, hard way to life and to avoid the wide gate and the wide, easy way that leads to destruction (Matthew 7:13–14) echoes the teaching of the father in Proverbs.

5 Sex

Proverbs 5

In this lesson (see also Proverbs 7) the father addresses the third major motivation for doing evil – sex. He begins by describing the attractions and dangers of illicit sex. There is a double meaning in verses 3 and 5. The imagery of verse 3a is used in Song of Songs (4:11) of kissing, and the word translated as 'speech' means 'palate', so the verse can refer to intimate kissing. In Hebrew, 'feet' can be a euphemism for the sexual organs. There are echoes of this two-way metaphor in verses 5–6, making it clear that sexual promiscuity is a temptation to desert the right path. It is not difficult to transpose the sweet-talking prostitute with the sweet-talking man looking for a one-night stand.

A list of negative consequences of sexual promiscuity follows as a motivation for rejecting the temptation (vv. 9–14): loss of social standing, economic complications and loss, health problems and deep personal regrets. Because the social mores and laws of ancient Israel lie behind verses 9–10 and 14, there is need here for cultural transposition into our society today. Sexually transmitted diseases are referred to in other ancient Near Eastern literature and are probably hinted at in verse 11.

As a positive motivation for sexual faithfulness, the father extols the joys of sex within marriage, the context within which God intended it to be enjoyed (vv. 15–20). The use of water imagery of life and joy is common in the Old Testament, because in Canaan fertility depended on the seasonal rains to fill the cisterns and replenish the aquifers that fed wells and streams. These verses have similarities with the erotic language used in the Song of Songs. This lesson is not prudish about sex when it is enjoyed in the right context.

It ends by taking up the two-way imagery, confirming that sexual temptation is a specific example of the discipline needed and life choice that has to be made in order to stay on the right path (vv. 21–23). The son's words of regret make clear that we have to take personal responsibility for this. The ultimate motivation for moral behaviour is that we are answerable to God. It is hypocritical to pray 'lead us not into temptation' without taking active steps to avoid it (v. 8) and resist it (v. 15).

6 Wisdom, creation and revelation

Proverbs 8

Personified wisdom provides a counterpart to the prostitute of Proverbs 5 and 7, with her seductive and deceitful words addressed to her victim. Here, in verses 1–21, wisdom addresses everyone in public with words of truth. She hates evil and epitomises the fear of the Lord. As well as bestowing material wealth and success, she gives the righteousness and justice that prevents its misuse. Those who rule rightly and justly do so by the wisdom she gives. That is why wisdom is more valuable than wealth and is to be pursued instead of wealth.

In verses 22–31, the focus changes to the Lord, who is the subject of all the active verbs. Wisdom's status is defined in relation to him. She is depicted as his child, having an intimate relationship with him. She was brought into existence – the picture used is that of birth – before everything else and so has precedence over all creation. Wisdom was at the creator's side as everything was created, and she delighted in all that was made, especially in humankind. Having been present throughout the process of creation, she knows the principles and plans used in creation. This gives her a unique knowledge of how it works, which fits her to be the mediator between the creator and humans, teaching them how to live rightly in his creation. This is the basis of the closing appeal to seek wisdom daily and to live by her instruction (vv. 32–36).

There were three sources of authoritative teaching in ancient Israel: the priestly law, the prophetic word and the counsel of the wise (Jeremiah 18:18). The wisdom teaching of the Old Testament has much in common with that found in the wisdom literature of ancient Egypt and Mesopotamia, which predates it by centuries. This is not surprising: knowledge of God can be gained from contemplating his creation (Psalm 19:1–4; Romans 1:20); humans made in God's image have some innate knowledge of right and wrong (Romans 2:14–15). The experience of learning to cope with life in God's world can result in insights into true wisdom. Genuine seekers after truth can learn from wisdom speaking through creation, conscience and experience. Of course, these insights must be tested and understood within the fear of the Lord taught in scripture if we are to use them as godly wisdom.

Guidelines

- How seriously is mentoring taken in the church today? In the theological college where I taught, we encouraged our students to adopt the practice of having a 'spiritual director' or mentor who would help them in their spiritual growth. When they left college and moved into positions of church leadership, we encouraged them to continue with this practice, finding a spiritual director outside their church situation. Some Christian organisations and denominations now run training programmes for spiritual directors and can put people in touch with those who have been trained. Mentoring should also be encouraged within the fellowship of the church in both formal and informal ways. It is an obvious need for those who are young either in years or in the faith, but all can benefit from it.

- As we have seen, the primary concern in Proverbs is with the formation of a godly character. The kind of person you are determines what you do with your gifts and material resources. Many churches have programmes for training in various skills, such as worship-leading, leading small groups and methods of evangelism. Few have programmes centred on godly character formation as central to discipleship training. What do you think such a programme should look like? Could you raise this issue in your church? Of course, practical teaching to help in godly character formation should be part of the general preaching and teaching programme of the church.

- If money, power and sex are major motivations for doing evil, they clearly ought to be subjects covered in the church's teaching programme. It would be good to follow the example of the father in Proverbs 5 and present the positive benefits of these good gifts as a motivation for their right use and not dwell solely on the negative motivation of the dangers they present when given into as temptations to do wrong. Some questions to ponder:

  - What part do these motivations play in your life?
  - What other motivations are important for you? How might they lead you on to the wrong path in life?
  - 1 Peter 5:1–4 warns church leaders about the danger of the attractions of money and power as motivations for leadership. To what positive motivation does he point? If you are in a position of leadership, prayerfully ponder Peter's words.

1 God

Proverbs 16:1–9

God is mentioned in more than 60 proverbs in Proverbs 10—29. Nearly all these references use the personal name of the covenant God of Israel, Yahweh ('the Lord' in the NRSV). There is an implicit monotheism in Proverbs. No other god is mentioned. We are going to be looking at some of the verses that refer to the Lord, and which express some of the key things which Proverbs has to say about God.

God is the creator of everything (v. 4), but the emphasis in Proverbs 10—29 is that he is the 'maker' (the term used in these chapters) of humans (22:2) and their capabilities (20:12). Because he is the creator, God is transcendent. This is expressed in terms of his 'eyes' being present everywhere (15:3) and his knowledge of people's inner thoughts (24:10-12) and motives (v. 2). As a result, humans are subject to, and dependent on, him (vv. 1-3, 9). However, God is not detached from the world; he is active and involved in it. This is particularly expressed in terms of God's concern for social justice. As in the rest of the Old Testament, God is presented as the protector of those who are defenceless and on the edge of society: the poor (22:22-23), the widow (15:25) and the orphan (23:10-11).

Those who fear God avoid evil (v. 6) because God hates evil. Ten proverbs in Proverbs 10—29 concern things which are 'an abomination' to the Lord. Some are quite general: the way of the wicked and their thoughts (15:9, 26) or a crooked heart (11:20). More specific are lying lips (12:22), arrogance (v. 5), hypocritical worship (15:8), perversion of justice (17:15) and corrupt commercial practice (11:1). Sometimes there is a balancing statement about what 'delights' him (11:1, 20; 12:22). Those who do evil are warned that 'they will not go unpunished' (v. 5).

We must base our lives on what follows from these truths. We should recognise God's superior knowledge and power (vv. 1-4, 9) and submit to his instruction and wisdom (15:33). This means fearing the Lord and committing ourselves to him (15:33; 16:3, 6-9). The essential principle for coping successfully with life is summed up in verse 3: 'Commit your work to the Lord, and your plans will be established.'

2 Spirituality

Proverbs 23:15–18

'Spirituality' has a variety of meanings in postmodern western use. I will use it to mean 'the outworking in real life of a person's religious faith'. Proverbs deals with mundane, down-to-earth situations; topics that one might expect to appear in a handbook on spirituality, such as prayer, sacrifice and vows, rarely appear in it. Only about a tenth of the verses explicitly mention God. As a result, some scholars suggest that Proverbs is fundamentally a 'secular' book, with only a veneer of piety. This undervalues the repeated assertion in Proverbs that 'the fear of the Lord' is fundamental to wisdom. It is significant that it occurs in 15:33, which is close to the midpoint of the book. Deuteronomy 10:12–13 is the classic statement about the fear of the Lord. In essence, it is loyalty and love for God, shown in obedience to God's commands. In Proverbs, emphasis is put on the ethical aspect of this (16:6).

We saw last week that, in Proverbs, the kind of person you are is more important than what you earn or own. The book is about character formation. In Proverbs 10—29, this can be seen in the frequent references to the 'heart'. The word is used metaphorically. In English, we link it primarily with our emotions. In Hebrew, it refers to the centre of a person's being and is especially linked with thinking, deciding and willing (14:33; 16:9, 23). Modern Bibles often translate it as 'mind'. The father's desire is that his son's heart should be wise and continue in the fear of the Lord (23:15–28). The Lord judges people not by their actions but by testing their heart (15:11; 17:3; 21:2; 24:10–12).

The apparent secularity of Proverbs arises from this focus on the formation of a godly character because it results in an integrated spirituality. In Proverbs, godliness pervades the whole of life, not just the obviously religious parts of it. It is to be expressed in relationships with one's family, friends, neighbours and enemies. It should affect one's attitude towards the rich, the poor and the disadvantaged in society. It will be expressed in how one behaves in business, the law courts and the corridors of power. There is no sacred–secular divide in Proverbs.

3 Parents and children

Because Proverbs is written from the viewpoint of a father addressing his son, it presents the marriage relationship from the male perspective. Gender transposition is not difficult. What is said in Proverbs 10—29 must be understood against the background of the picture of a personal, loving relationship in Proverbs 5:15–20. Proverbs 12:4 emphasises the importance of making a wise choice of a spouse. The crown imagery may allude to crowns worn by bride and groom in the wedding ceremony of the time. How a wife might bring 'shame' to her husband is not explained. This may be clarified in 14:1, where 'house' is a metaphor for the family. This proverb echoes 9:1, implying much about the potential of a wife's wisdom. Proverbs 2:17 probably speaks of marriage as a covenant relationship made before God. A good wife is certainly seen as a gift from God (18:22; 19:14). The only domestic trouble, apart from troublesome children, mentioned in Proverbs 10—29 is nagging (19:13; 27:15). Infidelity has been dealt with in 2:16–17 and 5:18–20.

Children are exhorted to heed their parents' discipline and teaching (13:1; 15:5; 23:22; 29:15 imply the mother's role in discipline). The need for discipline in training children is a common theme. The first part of 22:15 is often taken to imply that there is an innate folly in children, but it could be an implicit condition: 'If folly is bound up…' The proverbs mention various ways in which children may be wayward (10:5; 13:1; 15:20; 19:26; 20:20; 28:7; 29:3). The earlier a child is given good training, the better (13:24; 22:6). Children who respond positively to discipline become wise people, bringing joy to their parents (10:1; 15:20; 23:24–25; 29:3). The references to 'the rod' may seem harsh but must be balanced by the reasonable approach and affectionate tone of most of the father's words, especially in the lessons. The appropriate way to exercise discipline is another matter that needs cultural transposition.

Finally, Proverbs 20:7 places on parents the responsibility of setting their children a godly example by modelling righteous behaviour. If they do this, their children will have pride in them (17:6) and heed their teaching.

4 Brothers, friends and neighbours

Proverbs 25:7c–10, 17–18

Few proverbs mention brothers, and the Hebrew word for 'brother' can refer to cousins or more distant relatives. The basic assumption is that brothers will come into their own in difficult times (17:17). However, they do not always live up to this, especially regarding poor relatives (19:7 – a proverb where 'brothers' probably refers to relatives in general). Proverbs warns against the intractability of family feuds (18:19; see also 6:19). The exact meaning of 27:10 is unclear; it may be encouraging turning for help to a nearby friend rather than a distant brother.

Hebrew uses the same word for 'friend' and 'neighbour'. The meaning must be decided according to the context. A friend is someone with whom there is some emotional attachment, whereas a neighbour is simply close spatially. Proverbs knows about 'the neighbour from hell' (21:10). The problem may be slander (11:9), which can lead to perjury in court (24:28; 25:18). The behaviour of some neighbours is stupid or thoughtless rather than malicious (26:18–19), though this probably destroys good personal relationships anyway. Proverbs warns against thoughtlessly imposing on your neighbour's time and hospitality (v. 17) or being a noisy neighbour (27:14), even when the intention is good. Good neighbours seek to create and promote community harmony. They know when remaining silent is wiser than criticising (11:12) and do not mislead by flattery (29:5). They seek to settle disputes by negotiation rather than legal action (vv. 7c–10). They are kind to those in need whom others may despise (14:20–21).

There are fair-weather friends, only concerned with what they can gain from the friendship (14:20; 18:24; 19:4, 6). Therefore true friends need to be cultivated, not neglected (27:10a). A true friend is faithful and constant (17:17) and some are more reliable than close family (18:24). Cultivating friendship requires a willingness to overlook occasional failings in the other and avoiding gossiping about them (17:9). Good friendship involves healthy debate, which sharpens wits and ideas (27:17). A good friend is prepared to say things that are true but may initially be hurtful (27:5–6). Hopefully, they will later be thanked for it (28:23) and the friendship be deepened.

5 Words

The category of sins mentioned most often in Proverbs is sins of speech. 'Lying lips are an abomination to the Lord' (v. 22). Maybe this is because speech plays a crucial role in the formation and development of social relationships. The development of a community requires good, reliable communication. Also, the God of Israel is a God who spoke to and with his people (Hebrews 1:1–2). The fullest revelation of God has come in the form of the Word made flesh (John 1:14). Speech plays a crucial role in developing our relationship with God.

In Proverbs, words are said to be powerful, imparting life and death. This is true both metaphorically of well-being in life (13:14; 15:4) and literally in the case of a witness in court where the death penalty may apply (14:25; 25:18). The ultimate origin of speech is a person's 'heart'. As we have seen, this is the centre of their being, especially the mind and will (15:7; 16:23). Therefore, a person's speech is an expression of their character. The intimate connection between a person and their words is emphasised in Proverbs by the frequent use of the body parts 'mouth/lips/tongue' to refer to words and speech rather than abstract terms.

Wise words are, most fundamentally, honest and true (v. 17). The purpose of the section of Proverbs entitled 'Sayings of the Wise' is to promote the use of such words (22:17). As far as Proverbs is concerned, with regard to words, fewer is better (10:19; 21:23). Speaking impulsively without restraint is the mark of a fool (29:20). This means that words should be used thoughtfully (15:28), which requires being a good listener before one speaks (18:13). Thoughtful speech is more likely to fit the occasion or person addressed so that it is a timely word which gives joy (15:23). Proverbs 25:11–12 uses striking and beautiful imagery of such words. In 16:21–23, the phrase 'increases persuasiveness' probably refers to the words being persuasive because they are well-presented ('sweet'). Persuasion also requires patience (25:15). Calmness and self-control are needed in the wise use of words (17:27; 14:29). Proverbs counsels against boasting about oneself and one's achievements (27:2). Humility marks the words of the wise.

6 Wealth and poverty

Wealth and poverty is a major theme in Proverbs and is more prominent here than in any other biblical book. Proverbs presents material prosperity as a gift from God that those who live by wisdom and the fear of the Lord can expect to enjoy (10:22; 14:24; 22:4). This is qualified by the warning that one's ultimate trust must be in God, not riches (11:4, 28). Most striking are the 'better than' sayings, which assert that commitment to God and moral virtue are more important than riches (15:16; 16:8, 16). Various particular virtues appear in 'better than' proverbs: love (15:17), humility (16:19), peaceability (17:1), a good reputation (22:1) and integrity (28:6). The wise will be ready to forego prosperity in order to follow God and to develop a godly character.

Proverbs is concerned with how wealth is acquired. The virtues listed above must not be sacrificed in pursuit of it. It should not be obtained by oppression of the poor (22:16; 28:8). A particular concern is get-rich-quick schemes (13:11; 20:21; 28:20, 22), presumably because of both the wrong attitude to wealth lying behind adopting such schemes and the likelihood of ignoring moral restraints in the rush to riches. Wealth should be gained by hard work (10:4; 12:27; 21:5) but one should not become a workaholic in pursuit of riches (23:4–5).

Although Proverbs warns that laziness leads to poverty, this is not a comment on poor people as a whole. The main reason why there are poor people in a society is social, economic and legal oppression (13:23; 22:7–8, 16, 22–23; 28:15; 30:14). Proverbs does not present a programme for eradication of poverty but provides a theological basis for one: God created the poor person as well as the rich (14:31; 17:5; 22:2; 29:13). To oppress poor people is to insult God, while recognising them as fully fellow human beings is to honour God. Proverbs calls for generosity towards poor people, which will alleviate their plight, and might do more than that (19:17; 21:13; 22:9; 28:27). The righteous person should know, and by implication uphold, the rights of the poor (29:7, 14).

Guidelines

Each of the themes considered this week could profitably be made the subject of further personal pondering or group discussion. Here are some comments to stimulate further thought.

- Consider the things said to be 'an abomination to the Lord'. What priority would you give to them as social evils that need to be eradicated? Are there other things that you think should have equal or greater priority in your society today?

- How integrated is your spirituality? What about the spirituality taught in your church? A school teacher commented that, because she taught a small Sunday school class, she was asked to come forward in church and be prayed for, but the church never prayed for her because she taught a few hundred children in the local secondary school. This showed an implicit sacred–secular divide.

- We hear a lot about dysfunctional families today. It is clear from Proverbs that 'elder abuse' is not something new. Not everyone is married or a parent, but we are all children. What can Christians, individually and collectively, do to promote functional families?

- I was asked to preach on 'Being a good neighbour' as part of a series a church was doing on 'Creating good communities'. Proverbs was a good resource for this. What other topics would you include in such a series?

- Most people today get the impression that the church, and therefore the Bible, is obsessed with sexual sins. However, what is true of Proverbs is true of the Bible as a whole: the most commonly mentioned sins are sins of speech. How seriously do you take that? Is it reflected in the teaching of your church? James 3:1–12 is an important passage about the use of speech addressed to those with teaching responsibility in the church.

- Despite internationally agreed goals to reduce poverty, there is a growing poverty gap between and within nations. Taking up Proverb's theological basis for concern about poor people and its insights about the causes of poverty and the importance of generosity towards those in need, can you think of a practical project for combating poverty in your community – or is there one already in operation that you could support?

FURTHER READING

R.J. Clifford, *Proverbs (Old Testament Library)* (John Knox Press, 1999).

Ernest Lucas, *Exploring the Old Testament: Volume 3: The Psalms and wisdom literature* (SPCK, 2003), chapters 3–4.

Ernest Lucas, *Proverbs (Two Horizons Old Testament Commentary)* (Eerdmans, 2015).

R.C. Van Leeuwen, *Proverbs (New Interpreter's Bible, Volume 5)* (Abingdon Press, 1997).

Deuteronomy 1—10

Jenni Williams

Deuteronomy is a book about time – not time in the abstract, but time in the story of God and his people. It begins at a specific point in the narrative of Israel's journey: their entry into the land. It is likely that Deuteronomy was beginning to be shaped at another dramatic point in historical time: the rediscovery of the 'book of the Law' (2 Kings 22—23). Scholars believe that what was found was an early core of Deuteronomy, perhaps chapters 12—26, which then grew to meet the need in the light of Josiah's reforms. It probably took its final form in the post-exilic period.

To that extent, therefore, Deuteronomy is a perfect example of contextual theology. A time of dramatic religious reform and the realisation of God's judgement on unfaithfulness explain the urgency in Deuteronomy of faithful remembering. An anxiety about the future (from Moses' perspective) exactly explains what Josiah's concerns were. Deuteronomy reaches past the time of Moses to reflect on a society settled in the land where ancient tribal ties become adherence to the local 'city', where authority is devolved and therefore where the possibilities of other beliefs and practices creeping in becomes a real anxiety. Deuteronomy, then, is the place where past, present and future intertwine. The passages chosen reflect both this looking back and looking forwards.

There is considerable discussion over whether Deuteronomy articulates philosophical monotheism (that is, it claims there exists only one god) or whether it argues for an exclusive henotheism (that is, it acknowledges the existence of other gods but demands an absolute loyalty to this one). The passages we will be looking at over the next two weeks demonstrate for us what is often called 'practical monotheism'. In the light of the exodus, it is clear to Israel whom they must worship: the Lord, who is both creator and saviour.

Unless otherwise stated, Bible quotations are from the New Revised Standard Version (Anglicised).

1 Long enough in the past

Deuteronomy 1:1–36

Deuteronomy has what might seem a clunky beginning: the announcement of a speech by Moses immediately followed by four and a half verses of history and geography! In fact, this is the perfect key to understanding where the book is headed: a restatement of the law with a retelling of salvation, past and ongoing, as a guide for the future in the land.

The Lord is named carefully in this passage as 'YHWH our God'. This is the language of the covenant. The Lord's first words to Israel say literally, 'It is enough for you stopping on this mountain.' This can be a neutral expression (as 2:3) or a negative one (3:26), but it's certainly brisk. The past is over; it's time to move, time to look to the future.

Then comes another apparent interruption: Moses' complaint about his workload. In fact, this too is about how the past, the present and the future intertwine. In the past, the Lord promised that the Israelites would be as numerous as the stars (Genesis 15:5). They are now, if not yet that numerous, certainly many more than they used to be, and Deuteronomy 28 promises that if they follow the Lord they will remain many in the land. But as they scatter and settle into smaller units, it will be even more important than it was in the desert to have appropriate, just leadership. The one-leader model has already been outgrown and Moses' words reach forwards to the land.

Moses then goes on to recount past failures at some length, because they still impact on the present and point forwards to the future. Israel was intimidated by enemies instead of trusting in God. This led to a disobedience, which is why they are where they are (the wilderness) at this point in time. But this is also the story of Israel in the land: not trusting the Lord. Once in the land, this distrust takes another form: turning to other gods for help in the face of danger (or even in times of prosperity). It is about this risk that the rest of Deuteronomy shows the greatest anxiety – understandably, given Josiah's need to reform a religion that had become mixed up with other gods. The exilic and post-exilic understanding of the fall of Israel and Judah is connected to this idea (prophets like Jeremiah are a good example of this).

2 Moving on

Some scholars argue that Deuteronomy contains three sermons from Moses; this passage is the beginning of the second sermon. Yet it begins with a connective: 'So now, Israel' (v. 1). In the light of the past (the Lord's faithfulness and Israel's disobedience), what needs to happen now (keeping the Torah) will bring future blessings (a great nation with wise laws will be seen as proof of a God who has a close relationship with his worshippers; see v. 6).

Uniqueness is a major part of this passage's focus. A god who hears his worshippers when they call is not always a given in the ancient world (v. 7). The people are encouraged to understand the uniqueness of their God and their relationship with him: no other god has ever had such an intimate relationship with his people and answered them so reliably. The Torah is thus a unique law code which marks a unique relationship.

Of course, other ancient law codes claim divine inspiration. In this one, however, relationship is intimately bound up with the law for everybody, not just kings or leaders, as was more usual. It may seem odd to insist that nothing should be added to what Moses is commanding, when Deuteronomy itself contains many laws which clearly reach forwards. Some scholars have suggested that Deuteronomy is essentially a development or expansion of the laws in the decalogue (see day 4). If so, then the subsequent case law is not an addition but to be understood as application in a given context.

Another useful perspective comes from ancient Near Eastern law codes, which often have a provision that the king's law (or a treaty) cannot be changed without the agreement of both parties. Thus, Deuteronomy could indeed present an evolution in the law, but one of God's approving. We can see an example of this in the appointing of the elders or the law on inheritance in Numbers 27. So the covenant cannot simply be altered for Israel's convenience; it can evolve at the Lord's initiation, but it stands.

3 Future forgetting

This passage reveals the greatest anxiety of Deuteronomy: that Israel might forget who has saved them and make an idol. The people of Israel in the timeline of the narrative were about to face the challenge of encountering different peoples with different gods. Deuteronomy itself can be understood as shaped like a covenant document, and its major theme is absolute faithfulness to the Lord in the covenant relationship. The long history of Israel in the monarchical period is the story of a people struggling and often failing to stay committed to their God.

Nothing in creation is to be worshipped. In the nations around Israel, there were deities related to the sun, the moon and the stars. The majesty of the night sky makes it easy to understand why people would have worshipped these extraordinary lights, and indeed, when everything depends on the sun, it's easy to understand why it too would be worshipped. But Deuteronomy argues that creation must not be worshipped. The reason given is that the Lord does not self-reveal visually: verse 15 reminds them that although the Lord spoke, he was not seen. The psalmist reminds us that creation witnesses to the Lord's works, but Deuteronomy insists that this cannot be how he is to be articulated. The repeated use of 'fire' (vv. 15, 24) links to the exodus event, where fire guides the people and hence is a symbol of the Lord's presence. However, it also powerfully symbolises holiness, purity and awe.

Idols not only represent the divine but have some form of power or connection: they are the god they depict. Because these things cannot save or really do anything at all, they are not to be confused with the God who brought Israel out of Egypt (v. 20). Similar ideas can be found in Isaiah 45 or Psalm 115, both of which contain the fully articulated idea that idols are worthless to worship: that is, they are not gods because there are no other gods. Deuteronomy does not articulate this view as such, but it does clearly warn that only the God who saved Israel is to be worshipped. Explicitly, it talks of complacency in the land, implying that when people become comfortable it is easy for them to forget and then fall away from their faith.

4 The eternal 'today'

Deuteronomy 5:1–12

The text of the 'ten words' (not 'commandments' in the Hebrew) is one of the most familiar in Jewish and Christian spirituality. In the book of Exodus, the setting is immediate: the words are proclaimed on Sinai. In Deuteronomy, the words are a remembering, something from the past. But they are also very present.

First, we note the gathering of all Israel to hear Moses' speech. We might compare this with Josiah's gathering of the people (2 Kings 23:2) to hear the 'book of the covenant'. In that story, we are told that the king and all the people bound themselves to the covenant. Here, that idea is deepened and developed into an idea: verse 3 states that the Sinai covenant was not made with the people's ancestors (literally 'fathers') but with the people who are being addressed by Moses at this point, by the Jordan. Historically, of course, this is not true: because of their constant lack of faith, the Sinai generation were forbidden to enter the land. But theologically, this statement conveys a hugely important idea: each generation is the one with whom the covenant has been made. If we consider again the story in 2 Kings 23, we can see the importance of this theological perspective, often called 'actualising'. Their loyalty to the Lord must be theirs, not that of their parents.

Some traditions argue that the first of the words is a statement of who it is the people must be loyal to: that is, verse 6 by itself. We note again the insistence on the exodus as epitomising who God is. The instruction which follows the idea reads that they must not have any other gods 'before my face'. Again, as we saw above, this might mean there aren't any or, more likely, it means Israel must not treat anything else as an object of worship.

The Lord's self-description as a 'jealous' God can seem troubling. However, a plausible way to interpret this idea relates to the older English usage of the word 'jealous': not to denote an irrational emotion but rather the just insistence of one's rights. The Lord is 'jealous' of his right to exclusive devotion; hence he does not tolerate anyone infringing this right. (On the matter of the generations, see day 6.)

5   Revering the Lord: his name and his day

Deuteronomy 5:11–15

The question of misusing the Lord's name (literally, 'take up the Lord's name to worthlessness') is often understood by Christians merely as a bar to using the Lord's name as an expletive. In fact, it is addressing a far graver issue: the misuse of the Lord's name in either magic or to pronounce a curse that he has not instructed, misuse that can be part of the abuse of power. It can also be concerned with the swearing of an oath about something that simply does not deserve this degree of gravity, or where the oath-taker has no intention of keeping their oath.

The sabbath commandment provides a bridge between the words about how Israel is to understand God and how Israel is to behave towards each other. In the book of Exodus, the reason given for the sabbath is God's day of rest in Genesis 2:3. This makes it all the more striking that Deuteronomy should use the exodus event as its explanation of the sabbath. This relates to what we have seen about how Deuteronomy articulates the nature of God as saviour. The book of Exodus simply notes that a slave should be allowed a sabbath, whereas Deuteronomy appeals to Israel's release from slavery in Egypt as the reason why they should be allowed a sabbath. This is in keeping with the social justice laws throughout the rest of Deuteronomy, many of which appeal to Israel's experience of being enslaved in Egypt as a spur not to act as oppressors themselves. The commands illustrate how Israel was to think of itself: as a community of saved people.

6 Each other in the past, present and future

Deuteronomy 5:16–22

The command for children to honour father and mother is connected by Duane L. Christensen to the rather troubling observation in 5:9 about the Lord punishing to the third or fourth generation (although the contrast with the duration of generations to whom he shows love should not be over-looked). He argues that parents must teach their children rightly about God so the household (three or four generations in those days) does not face punishment and disaster. Children thence repay their parents, who ensured the Lord's blessing in their good teaching, by honouring them. This honour would be material: in a society with very little social care infrastructure, children must look after their elders.

To take the life of another is to infringe on God's prerogative as life-giver and life-taker. Thus, although premeditated murder is part of the prohibition, it extends more broadly than this. For manslaughter, the killer is dealt with differently (by fleeing to a city of refuge; see 4:41–42).

Adultery is a fundamental boundary infringement in human relationships. Often interpreted in Christian circles as a blanket prohibition on many different forms of transgressive sexual activity, the instruction here is narrow and specific: sexual contact with a woman already in an established sexual relationship with another man.

The stealing prohibition is sometimes understood as kidnapping: the removal of a member of the family in a small subsistence household would be catastrophic. But overall, we may observe that theft of anything when people have very little is a huge disaster.

Likewise, in any society where little is written down, people must be able to trust each other's promises. This is what makes the need to resist giving false reports such a priority.

Desiring what someone else has is destructive. Men are warned not to 'covet' their neighbour's wife. The verb here can have an overtone of pandering to one's own desire and trying to find a way to bring that to fulfilment. As such, it reaches beyond simply finding someone attractive, into a socially destructive scheming for what one wants. The material possessions of other people have a different verb: possibly because a wife, although certainly under her husband's authority in that day and age, and with fewer rights than he had at that time, is not a possession in the same way.

Guidelines

Human beings are constrained by time. We forget. The writer of Deuteronomy, with his insistence on remembering and allowing that memory to feed forward into the future, challenges our discipleship.

George Santayana is credited with saying 'those who cannot remember the past are doomed to repeat it'. This encapsulates the anxieties of Deuteronomy for God's people. Faithfulness to the Lord and the resistance to placing other things in his place (which is a huge part of idolatry) are challenges all through our lives. We must always be wary of a tendency to make God like something (or someone) else and to make something (or someone) else God. We don't worship the sun, moon and stars, but how easily do we worship Christian superstars? We declare our wholehearted allegiance to God, but how easily do we put our real faith in preachers, political leaders and strategies – and fail to listen for the divine voice which calls us to follow him alone? Hearing the story of God and his people over and over again is the way we remember and correct where we have drifted.

> Lord, this week help me to remember that you alone are God. Help me to remember what you have done for us. Challenge me where I have put too much faith in what is not you. Amen

1 All day, every day

Deuteronomy 6:1–9

As chapter 6 opens, there is a clear articulation of the idea that for Israel to live long and happily in the land, they must keep the Torah: obedience to the commands brings the promise of long life in the good land, which is a pervasive theme in Deuteronomy, symbolising the Lord's favour and an indication of a righteous life. The combination 'commandments, statutes and ordinances' is a very deuteronomic way of expressing the Torah. There is no discernible difference between the three, but the combination of the ideas emphasises the fullness of what Torah is.

We may also note the element of conditionality that is attached to living long in the land. It is an indication of covenantal thinking: a covenant must be kept or it is nullified. It was the challenge to understand this that shows in the exilic prophecy of Isaiah 40, where the prophet must make the exiles realise that it was not the Lord who abandoned them or was too weak to save them. Rather, it was they who broke the covenant.

Then follows the Shema (Hebrew for 'hear'; vv. 4–9), which is linked to 5:1 by its repeated use of the word 'hear'. This is the great creedal statement in Deuteronomy, which explains the uniqueness of the Lord (one) and hence how utter the devotion of Israel must be: everything they are must be devoted to him. There is a lot of debate about what we should understand about 'oneness' here, related to the question of monotheism which we explored last week. Is he the only God, a 'oneness' within himself? Is it a way of avoiding localising deities, which was frequent ancient Near Eastern practice? In this way of talking, a god would be described as the god of their locale. As we have seen repeatedly, the Lord claims an absolute sovereignty over the whole of creation and therefore is not to be reduced to localising.

2 Future-proofing

Deuteronomy 6:17–25

The people are instructed to obedience with another triad of actions using covenant language (commandments, decrees, statutes). But this time, the commandment is much more present-based than future: verse 18's promise that if they do what is right they will be able to do the thing they should now be doing, which is following the earliest command in Deuteronomy ('resume your journey', 1:7). Obedience thus has a present and future dimension as well as a resonance with past disobedience. This present command also reminds them that now, just as much as ever, they must be obedient and trusting because there are enemies in the land.

However, we should not interpret this command to consequential obedience as 'earning salvation'. Verses 20–21 articulate clearly that the meaning of Torah is not to create a situation where the Lord will save them because they obey him. Rather, the meaning is that God has already saved them in the exodus. As such, their obedience will lead to continued walking in this salvation. This is the meaning of the Torah according to Deuteronomy: one might almost call it a theology of law. This distinction is important to remember and helps us better understand Jesus' speech with the Pharisees of his time. It also helps guards against a skewed perception of Judaism, often prevalent in the church. In this passage, the teaching is explained in all its fullness: the meaning of the laws is a salvation already given. The Torah is part of the Lord's good gift to his people in covenant.

The other significant aspect to note is that verses 21–25 have been thought by some scholars to be a very early creed, perhaps from some kind of liturgical setting. The idea of question and response does suggest some form of liturgy, but it also has a domestic flavour. Yesterday's reading encouraged parents to teach the Torah to their children, and this passage expects curious children to ask about what they are taught: an indication of a virtuous learning circle, but also strongly suggesting a private setting. Indeed, verses 20–21 are still part of a modern Jewish Seder done at home. By contrast, the festivals of Passover and Unleavened Bread come together in Deuteronomy as one public festival when Israel reaches the land. However we understand the liturgical function of this text, its focus on passing on, teaching and active learning remain front and centre.

3 A difficult command

Deuteronomy 7:1–11

This is, for Christians and Jews down the ages, one of the most difficult passages to encounter in Deuteronomy. The 'clearing away' of indigenous nations, together with the associated apparent wholesale slaughter, feels deeply repugnant, even immoral. Interpreters throughout history have approached this passage in different ways. Origen argued that this should be interpreted allegorically about utterly destroying the sins in one's own life. Other interpreters have argued that what is being instructed here is not genocide (that is, a racially or tribally motivated killing), since elsewhere in Deuteronomy foreigners are not only tolerated but to be welcomed into festivals and sabbaths. Moreover, it is argued, the motivation for the command is clearly articulated as the risk of turning away to other gods (v. 5). That said, it is clear that particular nations are targeted and in 9:4 it is described as the Lord's punishment on those nations for their wickedness. The problem is, no matter how wicked they may have been (and actually there is no reason to suppose they were more wicked than nations outside Canaan), no one could possibly countenance the idea of the execution of children for 'wickedness'.

Another way to approach this passage is to consider a) whether it ever actually happened, and b) whether it was ever meant to. In respect of the former, we may observe that in the book of Joshua, groups described as 'wiped out' appear a few chapters later (see Joshua 11 and 13). This then leads us to the question of the latter: what is even meant in this passage. There is reasonable evidence that the kind of wholesale wiping out described here is an ancient Near Eastern form of hyperbole, an exaggerated way of describing victory. For example, the victory stele (stone) of Merneptah and the Mesha stele from a Moabite king in the eighth century talk of Israel experiencing utter destruction. Since in neither case were the people of Israel (Merneptah) nor the northern kingdom (Mesha) literally destroyed, there seems a strong argument here. This would then explain the puzzle of verse 3: if a nation is to be literally utterly destroyed, there seems no need then to insist on not marrying among them. There are further helpful discussions in the 'Further Reading' list.

The text remains deeply problematic and unsettling but perhaps can be set into a frame whereby it can never be used as a justification for genocide. One other thing to note before we leave this difficult text: Israel is reminded that, although they are now a numerous people as we saw in 1:10, they were not chosen at the point of being numerous. No matter how they now flourish, they were chosen at a point of weakness and non-flourishing. Moreover, the same fate is threatened to Israel if they become unfaithful (8:20).

4 Warnings against getting comfortable

Deuteronomy 8:11–20

This passage encapsulates the major pastoral anxiety of Deuteronomy: complacency. We saw above that the outworking of complacency is unfaithfulness to the Lord. This passage traces the pattern of how complacency plays out: becoming comfortable in the material sense (v. 12), seeing prosperity (v. 13) and beginning to feel that this is all somehow deserved (v. 14).

The flow breaks at this point to rehearse the Lord's provision for the people at a time of material want and in real danger in hostile environments. Verses 15–16 describe known desert hazards. The point made is that the way they survived was not by the knowledge and skills of desert people (by finding oases and so on), but rather by miraculous interventions by the Lord; they were completely dependent. They were even defended or healed from poisonous creatures. The use of the word 'seraphim' here (v. 15; literally 'burning ones') is intriguing. It recalls the episode in Numbers 21:6–9 where miraculous healing comes from a punishment of being bitten by snakes, but is also used in Isaiah 6 to describe the creatures which fly above the Lord in the heavenly realms. It thus has a definite idea of the miraculous in it even, though snakes are everyday creatures.

Water comes from a 'flint rock' (v. 15; not a place water flows). The Lord feeds the people with something they've not known, not ordinary bread but something miraculous (v. 16; its name, 'manna', comes from the Hebrew meaning 'What?'). The purpose was to humble and test them, that is, to teach them dependence and obedience but also to bring about a positive outcome for them.

Then the speech returns from the lessons of past difficulty to warnings against complacency: the belief that Israel has somehow achieved what it has by itself (v. 17). This is to forget their need of the Lord and will lead to unfaithfulness and ignoring the Torah (v. 11); the covenant will be broken and the relationship effectively made no different from the way the Lord sees other nations. The 'treasured possession' (7:6) will become just another nation (v. 20). The root cause of this complacency which leads to disaster is forgetting, hence the urgency of the command to remember.

From the point of view of those who put Deuteronomy together, this passage can be understood as a theological reflection on exactly what did happen: forgetting, material comfort, a sense of deserving instead of grace, a sense of independence from the Lord, adopting other gods (without necessarily abandoning the Lord) and, in consequence, disaster.

5 No better in the past, so watch the future

Deuteronomy 9:4–29

This passage retells an important story which points forwards. It begins with another reiteration hat the land is an undeserved gift and then follows with an illustration from the past. In chapter 7, Israel were reminded that it was not because they were flourishing that they were chosen. This time, they are reminded that they were not chosen because they were more meritorious than any other nation. So the warning to Israel is stark: the Canaanites will lose the land for being wicked, and Israel's record is not impressive in faithfulness. Thus the fate of Canaan becomes the threat to Israel if they do not follow the Lord's commands.

The absence of Moses caused a loss of faith among the people. While Moses was on Sinai, his encounter with the Lord was fundamental for the people's relationship with the Lord. But here, the story is told as another instance of Israel's unfaithfulness. The making of the golden calf is complex. It was probably intended not as a rival to the Lord but rather to function as a representation of him, perhaps even a reassurance in the absence of Moses (Exodus 32:1). But, as we have seen, the ban on such representation in Deuteronomy is absolute.

Moses describes his two fasts, of which the second was apparently an act of representative repentance. It underlines Moses' intercessory ministry for Israel. Describing this episode here links back to the ten words and their importance, by emphasising the forgiveness and intercession needed for the idol. But it also looks forwards to a time when Israel will have to do without Moses permanently, even as they were once without him temporarily. In this sense, the retelling of a past episode becomes absolutely future-situated.

The chapter concludes with another story along the same lines, of Israel's disobedience and Moses' intercessory role. Moses' plea is predicated on the Lord's nature as such; its function is to explain why the Lord relents when Israel consistently fails to live up to the covenant.

6 Past mercy, future living out

The story continues as the disasters of unfaithfulness in the preceding verses give way to an experience of mercy and a fresh start as two new stone tablets were made. The fact that the replacement tablets have the same words on them emphasises that the covenant is restored, not lost or modified. In view of the insistence we saw in 4:2, this emphasis is significant. And in considering the reforms under Josiah and the call back to the covenant, the emphasis on reform (in this case literally re-forming) rather than innovation comes to the fore. The focus now, though, is on how the worship practices of Israel developed. This links back to Moses' role as intercessor, which prefigures the priests from the line of Levi.

Then, like all skilful preachers, Moses loops back to the main point: in view of the story of Israel's failures and the Lord's graciousness and mercy, what does the covenant he gave ask of them? Micah's answer to the same question (Micah 6:8) is perhaps better known, but Deuteronomy's answer encapsulates everything we have been exploring (vv. 12–13). What is required is utter commitment, keeping to the Torah, and what is promised is the benefits of doing so. Verse 14 uses a sort of reiterative wordplay to emphasise the Lord's absolute sovereignty in the divine realm: the 'heaven of heavens' can be understood to mean the very essence of heaven itself. The Lord is absolutely sovereign over the cosmos, even the parts of it to which human beings cannot aspire, as well as the parts to which they are allotted (the earth and all that is in it).

The commitment of Israel is to be an attitude of the 'heart' (v. 16). This is not to be understood as the place of emotions, but rather, in biblical thought, the place where decisions are made, where commitments are kept whether or not the emotions incline to them. To circumcise the heart is not to say that somehow they will all suddenly want to keep the covenant, but rather to say that they will choose to, even when they don't feel inclined to. The phrase is not to devalue physical circumcision, but to recognise that the heart must underpin the action. We might compare this to 5:2, where covenant cannot be inherited, or 5:21, where attitude of heart is important.

Guidelines

The Shema is used by Jesus to summarise the Torah, and he couples it with a command from Leviticus about other people (Matthew 22:37–39). Understanding who God truly is drives everything Christians are called to do. This may be rather obvious, but consider: the writer of Deuteronomy spends a lot of time discussing Israel's past failures. Thus there is a point to all this retrospection, as it emphasises the two aspects of faith: the importance of knowing God's nature and his relationship with his people, in particular that what God offers is undeserved and yet at the same time that his people are beloved and chosen and even 'treasured'.

Understanding the reality of our failures is not some obscure masochistic impulse; it should preserve us from arrogance and judgementalism. It should drive us to walk God's way, not because we earn something future through it, but rather because a past event – salvation – has forever changed our present and future to make us God's people. There can be no going back from that. A secure knowledge of our own belovedness should compel us outward to others, seeing them as they are: people loved by God.

Of course, as human beings, we fail to live up to this. But it should always be the benchmark of our discipleship, because then we understand God better and better. Not for nothing does Paul talk about seeing God 'face to face' (1 Corinthians 13:12): it emphasises the impossibility of humanity knowing him fully in this life, the promise of standing one day in his presence and the security of knowing that he already knows us utterly. But it also emphasises relationship with God in this life: it is not a hopeless longing for what we can never know. Therefore, to know ourselves as we truly are is to seek to see ourselves as God sees us. Until that day, Deuteronomy teaches us to seek always to stand, like Moses, on the mountain of God's word and see past, present and future as all encompassed in God's plan.

Lord, I long to know you as you are. While I wait for that day, help me to keep listening. Help me to see myself and others as you do. Amen.

FURTHER READING

Duane L. Christensen, *Word Biblical Commentary: Deuteronomy 1–11* (Word, 1991).

Philip Johnston, *Deuteronomy: The People's Bible Commentary* (BRF, 2005).

James Robson, *Honey from the Rock* (IVP, 2003).

Exaltation and abasement

Walter Moberly

'Celebrity' is one of the keywords of our culture. People in sport, music, film and television regularly receive astonishing money and adulation. Their exalted position can seem deeply enviable. Becoming such a celebrity is a strong aspiration for many, especially when young – despite the regularity with which those who are celebrities regret the media intrusions into their lives that come with the status. Roles that in principle involve service of others, from teaching to politics, tend to lack comparable attraction or glamour.

The underlying question (though not always recognised as such) is what counts as a good life. What does it mean to live well? What should our ambitions be? Or, put differently, what kind of memorial would we hope for when we die? For what (if anything) would we like to be remembered? How we answer this question – to which, of course, there is more than one good answer – will speak volumes about the kind of people we are and hope to be.

This question is central to the Bible – and the Bible's answers are astonishing. Despite a widespread popular perception that the Bible's answers are somewhat along the lines of 'Be good, be nice, keep your nose clean and go to church at least sometimes', anyone who reads the Bible carefully, and sets its answers alongside those that are prevalent in our culture, is likely to be surprised and disturbed.

Our readings this week will focus on one of the most characteristic ways in which the Bible approaches the question of what it means to live well and 'make it to the top'. The Bible's prime answer is succinctly summed in the words of Jesus, 'All who exalt themselves will be humbled, and those who humble themselves will be exalted' (Luke 14:11).

Unless otherwise stated, Bible quotations are from the New Revised Standard Version (Anglicised).

1 The song of Mary

Luke 1:46–55

Mary's song has been recognised as so important that it has received countless musical settings and features regularly in Christian liturgy. But familiarity and beautiful music, while good, always bring the danger that we become dull to what the words really mean.

Mary is a peasant woman living in Galilee, a poor and backward part of the Roman province of Judea, itself an awkward outpost of the Roman Empire. (The Romans were in Judea for strategic reasons, to help safeguard their control of the grain of Egypt, which fed people in Rome; they had little interest in the Jews as people.) Mary, though she hasn't yet had sex with her destined husband, has just become pregnant with a child who, according to the angel who spoke to her, is to be king over the Jewish people. (The Roman perspective on, or response to, this prospect was not mentioned.) Bewilderment would be a natural response. But Mary speaks with joy, using the idioms of Israel's songs of praise, both the psalms and the song of Hannah, Samuel's mother (1 Samuel 2:1–10).

God's singling out of a lowly – that is, poor and insignificant – woman as the mother of the coming king is the prime reason for her joy. God is not unduly concerned with status and recognition, worldly power or wealth. Rather, his priorities focus on those who respond truly to him: 'fearing God' in Hebrew idiom means responding rightly to God in trust and obedience (it has nothing to do with being frightened). God makes a nobody a somebody, and dismisses the seeming somebodies as nobody. And God is faithful to his promises, despite appearances to the contrary.

Strikingly, Mary speaks of this as accomplished fact. For some, this might induce cynicism about her words. If the emperor in Rome remained emperor, what had really changed? Yet Mary sees that God has his own priorities, which he implements in his own ways. She was not in a position to know that a Roman emperor would one day acknowledge her son as Lord, or that the priorities in life and death for countless millions beyond the Jewish people would be changed by this son. In her context, the words are vision and hope. In our post-Christian culture, the words must also be of vision and hope, a different way of looking at the world and of what really matters in life.

2 The vision of Isaiah

Isaiah 57:15; 6:1–8; 66:1–2; 52:13—53:12

The book of Isaiah is like a great choir: different voices singing the same harmonious song. In its various parts, the notes of exaltation and abasement are regularly sounded, and are central to the overall vision of the book.

A good keynote is 57:15. God is high and holy and inhabits eternity. That might make God sound distant or remote. But not so – this God is equally present in the human realm; though not just anywhere, but specifically with those who are lowly or humble, those who are not so full of themselves that they have no space for God. In theological terms, it is the paradox of transcendence and immanence. But we often miss the immanence, the presence, of God, because we do not know where to look, and look in the wrong place.

In the temple, Isaiah initially sees God as exalted and holy, 'high and lofty' (6:1). Yet again, this does not make God remote, for 'the whole earth is full of his glory' (6:3) – though one has to know where to look. When Isaiah abases himself because of his and his people's failure to speak of God rightly, God is there directly. Via a seraph, he cleanses the prophet so that he can speak rightly. A burning coal would be searingly painful. Yet Isaiah does not scream. Rather, he says that he is available to serve his Lord.

The final chapter of the book sounds a similar note. If God has made everything and inhabits heaven, he certainly cannot be 'contained' in any human construction, not even the temple in Jerusalem (66:1). But again, this does not make him remote. The supreme Lord is present with those who are poor, who may lack resources or human recognition, yet who are open and responsive to God and his priorities, and so are the object of his regard.

Finally, the passage about the suffering servant is well known, because of its obvious resonances with Jesus. But it has strong resonances within the book of Isaiah as well. Initially, we are shown a future state of the servant, exalted and high, as God is. But how will the servant attain this state? Only through faithfulness in suffering, and silent and patient integrity in the face of brutal opposition. An apparent road to oblivion is in reality the way to come to share in the exalted majesty of God.

3 Learning the hard way

Today, we will consider abasement and exaltation from a different angle.

Moses, the speaking voice throughout Deuteronomy, is giving basic instruction to Israel about what it means to be the covenant people of God. Here he focuses on the paradoxical problem posed by a good gift of God: the land of Israel, which is depicted in lyrical and glowing terms (vv. 7–9). That which is good may also be dangerous. Why?

Israel has spent 40 years in the desert. Although this arose because of a faithless failure to enter the promised land when God wanted them to (Numbers 13—14), Moses sees the divine judgement as a positive time also. God's purpose with Israel in the desert was to humble (abase) them and test them, with a view to better enabling their long-term obedience to God's ways (vv. 2–3). This humbling involved making things initially worse, 'letting you hunger', and then providing a solution, manna (which came daily and could not be stored; see Exodus 16), which was beyond anything they or their ancestors had encountered. This unprecedented experience was to teach them a deeper understanding of what it means to be human: humans are indeed material creatures with material needs, i.e. 'bread', but also creatures with a spiritual dimension who need to learn to live in obedient responsiveness to God (v. 3). The hardship of hunger and of living with the manna in the desert taught Israel this.

In the promised land, there is no manna, and good things are abundant (vv. 12–13). Yet this abundance, and the wealth that goes with it, brings a danger: that Israel may 'exalt' themselves (v. 14). This exalting is the opposite of their humbling, and it is a way of unlearning the lesson of the desert through no longer recognising God as key to their existence. They may simply ascribe their wealth to their own efforts, with no concern for recognising God's enabling of those efforts and providing the context for them. Thus they would reduce their understanding of the human to the merely material without the spiritual (vv. 17–18).

Hard times, times of humbling, can teach deep truths that may not be learned otherwise. It is a perennial danger, however, and one particularly acute in the wealthy west of today, to forget such wisdom through a self-exalting that is in reality no more than self-willed myopia.

4 How to misunderstand Jesus

The disciples of Jesus throughout the gospels are slow learners. When Jesus begins to teach them that his vocation under God involves suffering and dying – a deep humiliation – they don't know what to make of it. They just don't get it. Initially, Peter tries to correct Jesus, only to be given a stinging rebuke (Mark 8:31–33).

Jesus speaks of this again, with greater detail this time about the humiliation (mocking, spitting, flogging) on his way to being killed (vv. 33–34). But this is not what the disciples hear. They reckon that if Jesus is the Messiah, a king, then there is going to be a kingdom, and kingdoms have rulers and nobles who have power and authority over others. So James and John try to get in quickly. They ask for the top seats in the new kingdom over which Jesus will be king (v. 37). One can imagine Jesus replying with a heavy sigh, 'You do not know what you are asking' (v. 38). Because they are not listening to what Jesus is telling them about his vocation, they are thinking in entirely the wrong categories, which look like mere selfishness. While Jesus is speaking of being mocked and spat at, they are wondering how to get the best seats in the house.

The anger of the other disciples could be because of their fear that they might be losing out, if James and John have somehow got in first. So Jesus summons them all to give them some basic teaching. They know the familiar patterns of power and greatness. Yet if they are to follow Jesus, they must learn a completely different pattern: the great must be a servant; the person in top place must be a slave, that is, in bottom place (vv. 42–44). How can this be understood? Only by taking seriously the pattern of Jesus himself (v. 45). For only Jesus fully shows how this inversion of the ways of the world can make sense, and indeed reveal what truly matters in God's eyes.

People today still suppose that God, if he is really there, ought to fix the problems of the world in recognisable ways; Christians can be sucked into such suppositions also. To really learn that greatness lies in serving and giving oneself for others takes a long time, because it is such slow and painful lesson for most of us.

5 The way to greatness

In his passion, Jesus enacts what he taught.

When the Roman soldiers fix Jesus to the cross, Jesus is a figure of weakness, shame (he would be naked, despite the reverential loincloth of Christian art) and apparent complete failure. He is in extreme pain and faces imminent death. His situation and prospects are as low as they could be. Hence the unsympathetic mockery: if he is the Son of God, he must surely have divine power at his disposal (27:40). So let him demonstrate the reality of that role and power by somehow freeing himself from the instrument of his suffering and dying, the nails and the cross (27:42). For what use would that power be, if he cannot save himself from an otherwise hopeless situation? Indeed, the very reality of that role and power must be in doubt if he cannot save himself. So the religious authorities make Jesus the ultimate offer: if he will display his divine role and power by freeing himself from the cross, they, the accredited authorities of Israel, will here and now believe in him; Jesus will thereby fulfil the goal of his ministry. Hardly unreasonable, surely.

What do they get to see and hear? They hear Jesus cry out in agony and abandonment (27:46); he doesn't save himself, and neither does anyone else (such as Elijah) intervene. And so Jesus dies (27:50). The weakness and the failure are apparently complete, and the religious authorities know that Jesus is a loser.

Yet the final scene of the gospel portrays Jesus risen from the dead and telling his disciples that he has been given 'all authority in heaven and on earth' (28:18). The figure of utter weakness is now a figure of supreme power. How can this be? It is because Jesus gave everything, including himself, in the service of his Father that he has now received from his Father not only a life which is no longer subject to death, but also a supreme authority that relativises all other authorities. Jesus is now the sovereign Lord, in whom truth and power resides. Yet if the message of this Jesus, which his disciples are to give to the world, is to be true to him, it should not be enacted in any way other than that whereby Jesus himself enacted it. The self-giving that is integral to Jesus and his authority must be no less integral to his followers also.

6 Paul interprets Jesus

Philippians 2:5–11; 3:4–16

Paul instructs the Christians at Philippi in two distinct but complementary ways.

First, when speaking of how to live as a Christian, Paul appeals to the model of Jesus, that Christians should have 'the same mind' (2:5) as Jesus had. What was Jesus' mind? It was an understanding that equality with God, implicitly a position of supreme glory and authority, was not something to be exploited, in terms of using it for himself. Instead, it involved Jesus 'humbling' himself and being obedient to God without limit, that is, humbling himself even to a death of extreme shame and pain. The rightness of this is shown by God's response: that God has 'highly exalted' Jesus and made him the one whom everyone should recognise as 'Lord', the one who rightly claims allegiance and obedience in any quest to live life well. Paul in his own idiom retells Matthew's account of Jesus's death and resurrection, which we considered yesterday.

Second, a little further on in the letter, Paul gives what is in effect his personal testimony. He speaks initially of all the advantages he enjoyed as a faithful and observant Jew. Paul's tone is that of pride in good and valuable things, genuine privileges and advantages (3:4–6). Yet it is precisely these things of real value that he has been willing to set aside and count 'as loss'. Why? Because he has come to know Jesus – and knowing Jesus means living as Jesus did and replicating the pattern of Jesus. Paul enters into Jesus' sufferings, so that thereby he may also enter into Jesus' resurrection (3:7–11). That is, Paul restates in terms of his own experience the way of Jesus that he spelt out in the previous chapter. As Jesus laid aside all divine glory, to give himself in humble service, and God responded by exalting him, so Paul is laying aside all his human privileges and advantages and is giving himself in service, so that he also may receive the gift of resurrection life from God. To 'press on' in such a way is the vocation not only for Paul himself but for other Christians also (3:15).

The abasement and exaltation of Jesus has become the determinative picture of human life, and the determinative symbol for understanding God and God's ways and priorities.

Guidelines

We have looked hard this week at a basic and recurrent biblical concern. The theme of exaltation and abasement that is voiced by Mary in the Magnificat encapsulates something that runs through the Old Testament and is supremely realised by Jesus himself. This brings us back to our opening questions: what counts as a good life? What does it mean to live well?

Contemporary culture is full of alluring images of glamour and success, images that can be deeply seductive. We will all have felt their force in one way or another. To understand the Bible's different account of what makes life worthwhile, and what constitutes real exaltation, will never be easy and will demand much of us as Christians, as much in our corporate life as in our individual lives.

This time of Advent used to be a penitential season, parallel to Lent, to prepare us for Christmas as Lent prepares us for Easter. It is now a time of parties and carol services that seek to be upbeat and attractive. As we think of Christ in his first and second coming, what images should we have? We tend to romanticise the manger of Christmas, instead of seeing it as an anticipation of the cross, a symbol of poverty and ignominy. The second coming of Jesus is usually thought of as Jesus coming in glory. Yet the memorable portrayal of a final judgement that we find in Matthew's gospel, in Jesus' account of the sheep and the goats (Matthew 25:31–46) does not put the emphasis on Jesus on his throne of glory, even though this introduces the account. Rather, the emphasis is on what people did or did not do for the hungry, the thirsty, the stranger, the naked, the sick, the imprisoned – for that is where Jesus was, even if unrecognised.

How can we find ways, in our regular everyday circumstances, of seeking true exaltation from God? If people around mock or ignore, should we care? The question is how we should live so that one day we may hear God say to us, 'Good and faithful servant, well done.'

Eating together

Andrew Francis

The sharing of meals and food together is a vital part of the biblical witness. During these weeks which surround the 'turn of the year', as some of our village neighbours say, we journey from the season of Advent, into Christmas (through the new year) and then into Epiphany. It is a time of hospitality and the sharing of meals for many people.

So it is important for Christian believers to reflect upon some of the 'meal narratives' from our biblical heritage to listen for what God is saying to us through them. Both the Old and New Testaments reveal how the life of God's chosen people is predicated by shared meals; just think of the Passover (Exodus 12), the last supper (Matthew 26, etc.) or the first Christian communities (Acts 2:42–47). Many families and communities mark significant life events, not just birthdays, anniversaries, marriages or funerals but nearly every family gathering, with a shared meal. I know many congregations who have adopted a 'no meeting without eating' strategy.

As a writer, I keep rediscovering how many church leaders and theologians are exploring afresh how shared meals are helping reforge our contemporary witness.

How we prepare to welcome friends, neighbours and family or simply be others' guests challenges us to reflect spiritually why we are doing what we are doing. It is part of understanding our own 'holy habits'. I hope that in the following brief six subjects, caused by and explored through a particular biblical narrative, we can reflect upon our own faith, discipleship and how we celebrate as God's chosen people.

Each Bible passage is foundational for the reflection that follows. Unless otherwise stated, Bible quotations are from the New Revised Standard Version (Anglicised).

1 Christmas comes but once a year

Exodus 12:1–30

Christmas, Easter and Pentecost form the central tripod of Christian festivals, in which our Christian understanding of God and how God's deliverance is brought to us are celebrated. Just as Passover is the festival in which our Jewish sisters and brothers understand their deliverance, so Christmas, Easter and Pentecost's celebrations enable Christians to proclaim how the different persons of the Trinity enable our salvation. It is right that we celebrate Christmas but, unlike Passover, which demands a shared meal, the two gospel accounts of Jesus' birth do not. But in common with the central festivals of all world faiths, we recall and retell that narrative 'but once a year'.

This Passover narrative from Exodus is a mixture of instruction, history and theology. If God's chosen people follow divine instruction to bedeck their front doors (v. 7), feast together in specific ways (vv. 8–11) and acknowledging why they are doing this (v. 12), God's deliverance will be theirs (v. 13). The stewardship and feasting upon lamb are accompanied by the frugality in the eating of unleavened bread for the next seven days. Those who did not follow God's ways nor ate together in his prescribed manner were not spared from the anguish of ignoring the hope brought by God's deliverance (v. 19).

Having been privileged to join Jewish friends for their Passover meal, I was struck by their sincerity and spirituality: 'We can do no other than celebrate the source of our deliverance,' they told me. Is it too late for Christians to begin reclaiming Christmas and Jesus' birth as the source of our deliverance? The lesson from Passover is that the faithful of God do not forget – and, as many church posters declare, 'Jesus is the reason for the season.'

My early childhood was spent in 1950s Scotland, when Christmas Day was still just another day. The buses and trains ran, some shops opened and not all Christians could gather in church to sing carols because they had to go to work. Now we have bank holidays and winter holidays, when most of us are able to gather as Christians with time to celebrate the promise of the Bethlehem child, God's deliverance for all (John 3:16) and still have time to sit and eat with family friends and share our story of grace.

2 The promised land

Isaiah 65:13–25

In today's passage, Isaiah, as God's mouthpiece, issues due warning to the faithless that they will not enjoy the full fruits of God's blessing. They may try to celebrate and live life to the full, but it is those who are God's 'servants' (v. 13) who receive true blessing as they follow the ways of God's deliverance. How often do we see our more secular friends feeling that Christmas finishes with too much turkey and the dawning of Boxing Day? If they are the 'faithless' of this generation, how are we celebrating Jesus' coming well enough to be counted as God's servants?

The promised land of God is a state of blessing for all, as Isaiah reveals in verses 17 to 25, wonderfully subtitled 'The glorious new creation' (NRSV). In God's re-creation, the wrongs of the past are set aside. Clearly, much of Isaiah's God-given vision is apocalyptic and yet to be realised, for the sadnesses of this world, such as weeping (v. 19) and infant deaths (v. 20), continue. From verse 21, Isaiah is heard to be speaking about the fact that homes, communities, farms and daily work will be blessed.

My sister and I grew up in a poor Anabaptist pastor's family, in which our mother's gentle stewardship meant that we easily and wonderfully learned of the promise and provision of God. Saying grace, giving thanks, preceded every meal throughout the year. Psalm 23 ('You prepare a table before me…') reminded me that we never went hungry: there always was food on our table. Not everyone knew or knows that blessing.

However, Jesus' coming into God's world at Bethlehem is a time to declare that the promised land is on its way. The Messiah has come – and his reign is declared in the righting of wrongs. In our seasonal giving to food banks, or in the 24/7 opening of church premises for the homeless or as night shelters, we can declare that righting of wrongs. We share of our own blessings, in knowing Jesus the Messiah, as his servants. Past wrongs are set aside as we look to God before others call for our help. Now is the time for the outcast wolf to feed with the lambs of our own fold.

3 Meals which inflame our emotions

Luke 15:11–32

What do you call this hard-hitting parable of Jesus? Perhaps your age means that you automatically call it the parable of the prodigal son. But, increasingly, pastors, preachers and perhaps we ourselves recognise it as the parable of the angry brother or the forgiving father.

Why did Jesus tell this parable? Of course, it helps to amplify our understanding of the reign of God, when generosity and forgiveness must override the exclusion of the wayward, the spendthrift and the angry. At this time, how many households will ring to the exasperated cry, 'Why do *we* always have to have *your* cousin and family (or whoever) over to us?' How often do we entertain angels and are unaware of it?

John Koenig, the American theologian, in his book *Soul Banquets* (Morehouse, 2007), invites us creatively to affirm our emotions, whether positive or negative, about our seasonal hospitality and shared meals. The more I reflect upon this passage, the more I believe that this is a significant part of Jesus' intention, too, in telling this parable.

It is easy to understand the response of the angry brother; the frittering of a future inheritance by a sibling is more than frustrating. But is the anger directed at that – or at the provision of a feast and gifts for the returning brother? Do our Christmas and New Year frustrations cause our anger and tears because of similar things, or because we have been overambitious in our spending or giving? This parable calls us all to a fresh simplicity – from the gifts we give to the meals we prepare, so that we can give of ourselves wholeheartedly to those who gather with us.

Yes, I hadn't forgotten to mention the forgiving parent. Should he have seethed with anger or welcomed back his son? God so loved the world that he reconciled it afresh by sending Jesus the Son as the Bethlehem child (John 3:16). If we have no 'room in the inn' of our hearts during this Christmas season, we may be forcing others to become prodigals... and entrenching ourselves as 'angry brothers'.

4 Anointed or appointed?

John 12:1–8

Christians can act hypocritically; often, this is unintentional. One of the key mission questions that the church must wrestle with is how, in our growing post-Christian culture, can we facilitate believers' lifestyles to reveal Jesus-shaped discipleship?

We often discuss the Martha-and-Mary gospel passages and find in them an example of offering hospitality to both friend and stranger, in good times or sad. They always challenge our thinking.

Today's narrative tells us of a feast in their home, following Jesus' raising their brother Lazarus from the dead. Martha adopted her usual role of serving others, before Mary took a jar of expensive perfume and anointed Jesus' feet. Both gave important gifts, but Mary's was commented upon adversely by Judas Iscariot.

When does a gift become excessive? Judas wanted the perfume sold and the resulting money given to the poor; but John, this gospel's writer, knew Judas' real motive for his comments – personal greed. One can imagine how Judas soured the whole atmosphere of the party, belittling Mary's love and generosity, as well as Martha's hard work. Jesus rightly rebuked him.

Getting the balance right in declaring our love and devotion for Jesus is hard. There will always be men who sit back (regrettably) and women who are unacknowledged (sadly) for their hard work. There will be those whose gifts seem excessive, but they are well-intended and given with love. All these things should be done because we want to do them – not because of some misplaced sense of duty. How much of this is familiar in your family and household?

At Christmas, it is easy for the homes, lifestyle and behaviour of Christians to be so similar to that of non-believing, secularised friends and neighbours that we can fail to communicate the power, joy and simplicity of the Christian message. Now, I am not with the puritans – I enjoy helping the youngest family members decorate the tree, and I enjoy cooking Christmas dinner for all – but we want our Christmas letters and cards to proclaim the birth of our Saviour. We want visitors to our home to know that the presence of the living Christ is vital to our hope and living – just like Martha and Mary.

5 'People will come from east and west...'

Luke 13:18-30

Today, two of Jesus' parables and a piece of his other teaching take our attention.

The parable of the mustard seed speaks about the kingdom of God. Elsewhere, I have written (*Shalom: The Jesus manifesto*, Paternoster, 2016, p. 27 onwards) that the equally well-translated phrase 'the reign of God' should be used by Christians today. God's reign comes from small beginnings – seeds of hope, an invitation or an act of kindness – reaching out into its larger, overarching purpose.

In my family, we bake much of our own bread, as everyone did during Jesus' earthly ministry. Every baker understands Jesus' use of the yeast analogy when describing the reign of God. Yeast transforms the mix of flour, water and salt into something greater – a risen loaf, which, once baked, feeds far more than its basic ingredients can. The influence and activity of the reign of God can seem imperceptible, yet it transforms the basic and everyday into the nourishing and eternal. What did Jesus say? 'I am the bread of life' (John 6:35). Enabling Jesus to become the yeast in our lives will transform our discipleship daily to proclaim the reign of God in word and deed.

The way of discipleship has a 'narrow door' (v. 24) and we should enter it while we can. There will be those who ignore Jesus' coming, and his instruction, preferring to feast and drink rather than listen to the messianic teaching of the reign of God. They will witness others from all over God's world, gathering to celebrate that reign of God, which will turn the world's values upside down when the last will be first and first will be last (v. 30).

We delight in sharing the bounty of God's provision with family, friends, neighbours and others. How and whom we gather with proclaims what we believe about the reign of God. Now, my sister gathers our ageing family on Boxing Day, 'from east and west, from north and south' (v. 29), for a Christmas meal around her large dining table: three or four generations, often with solo friends or neighbours joining the family party. From such mustard-seed invitations, others have discovered a faith for life!

6 'Do not forget to entertain strangers'

Hebrews 13:1–8

I live on the edge of a village, where a public footpath across the field behind my garden leads up to the Ridgeway – a long-distance path. In summer 2018's heat, a couple came to the back-garden gate, asking us to refill their water bottles to meet their accompanying grandchildren's thirst. Welcoming others can be unexpected.

The writer of the letter to the Hebrews is writing to the faithful – those who should know much of the way of discipleship. This chapter begins with a call to behave as family, demonstrating love, loyalty, welcome and hospitality to one another and our wider family. Later (v. 5), the readers are reminded that God is a loyal and faithful God who never leaves nor forsakes us. So God's people *should* live and behave according to God's pattern and reign.

This extends itself to the nature of our everyday lives in the purity of human relationships (v. 4) and forsaking a 'love of money' (v. 5). We must subdue our baser human desires to live as God wants. We know that 'the Lord is my helper' (v. 6) and we can be encouraged by the example of our best Christian leaders, who live as God requires (v. 7), imitating their discipleship. For God's new community of faith proclaims both the constancy and continual message that Jesus is the same 'yesterday and today and forever' (v. 8).

How we live as individual disciples or together in gatherings of the faithful, be that in homes, church buildings or cathedrals, tells of our faith in Jesus Christ. That must also spill over into the communities where we live, as well as in the shops, pubs, offices and schools which make up the fabric of everyday life. The gospel is good news, but our words and works must share it every day.

The New Testament has a continual injunction to offer hospitality: 'Do not neglect to show hospitality to strangers' (v. 2). Jesus said, 'When I was hungry, you gave me food, when I was thirsty, you gave me a drink' (see Matthew 25:35–40). Our village's life revolves around the willingness to 'entertain strangers', be they summer walkers from the Ridgeway or visitors at Christmas. Sharing life and food as Jesus wants is not rocket science.

Guidelines

The weeks around Christmas are full of family gatherings and celebration meals, and hospitality abounds, helping us all think and reflect upon the sharing of food in the biblical heritage. Offering hospitality and gathering others to the table is something many *Guidelines* readers are privileged to share in. But what we do and its implications and how we share of God's provision for us raises questions:

- What is our intention in offering hospitality and sharing meals?
- In what ways is our lifestyle challenged to a greater simplicity of sharing (rather than excess)?
- How can we share of God's largesse to us in planning to give more to food banks and homelessness projects?
- Whether it is with relatives or an isolated neighbour, how can we ensure there is 'room at the inn' for the lonely and lost at this time of giving and grace?
- Do we share our 'bread of life' all year around? If not, why not?

As we gather in the season from Advent to Epiphany, here is a prayer for the journey:

Living God, whose intention in creation is that all may share in your peace, provision and plenty, teach us to live in communities and homes of hospitality, that others may learn of your life, love and goodness, as we follow in the words, works and ways of Jesus, whose Spirit empowers our very being. Amen

---

FURTHER READING

Andrew Francis, *Eat, Pray, Tell: A relational approach to 21st-century mission* (BRF, 2018).

Andrew Francis, *Hospitality and Community after Christendom* (Paternoster, 2012).

Andrew Francis, *Shalom: The Jesus manifesto* (Paternoster, 2016).

John Koenig, *Soul Banquets* (Morehouse, 2007).

Andrew Roberts et al., *Holy Habits: Eating Together* (BRF, 2018). This series also has further *Eating Together* booklets of Bible Reflections and Group Studies (BRF, 2019), to which I have contributed.

Advent reflections on the story of Jesus' birth in Matthew

Andy Angel

Traditionally, Advent has been a time of reflection and preparation. Moving towards the annual celebration of the birth of Jesus Christ, we read his words and those of other New Testament writers who speak of his coming in glory. We remember that one day we will stand before his throne of judgement and grace, and we think through the implications of this for our lives today. As we move towards celebrating the coming of Jesus Christ as a baby, we prepare for celebrating the day on which Christ comes as the Lord of glory to establish peace and justice throughout the world.

Just as we take time during Advent to think through the prophecies surrounding Jesus' coming in glory, so Matthew reflects on Jesus' birth in terms of its fulfilment of prophecies (some identifiable and one from an unknown source). Each of the stories in this narrative of Jesus' birth cites a prophetic word: Isaiah 7:14 in Matthew 1:18–25; Micah 5:2 and 2 Samuel 5:2 in Matthew 2:1–12; Hosea 11:1 in Matthew 2:13–15; Jeremiah 31:15 in Matthew 2:16–18; and an unknown prophecy in Matthew 2:19–23. Matthew sees the whole story of God's people coming to a climax in the person and work of Jesus.

Matthew structures his narrative of Jesus' birth using the following pattern: an angel commands Joseph in a dream and he obeys (Matthew 1:18–25); Herod acts against the Messiah (Matthew 2:1–12); an angel commands Joseph in a dream and he obeys (Matthew 2:13–15); Herod acts against the Messiah (Matthew 2:16–18); an angel commands Joseph in a dream and he obeys (Matthew 2:19–23). The contrast between Joseph and Herod introduces a key theme for Matthew: how will we respond to God and his Messiah?

Bible quotations are my own translation.

1 A people of blessing

Matthew 1:1–17

Discovering our family line has become quite a big business, with internet sites and television programmes devoted to helping us discover our origins and so our identity. Our identity is important to us. While biblical genealogies like the one in this reading excite few people, something significant is going on in these first 17 verses of Matthew.

This genealogy reveals something of Jesus' identity. Jesus is 'the Messiah, the son of David, the son of Abraham' (v. 1). Matthew divides the genealogy into three blocks (v. 17): from Abraham to David, from David to Babylon and from Babylon to the Messiah. While it is unclear why Matthew counts 14 generations for each block (not least as the final block only has 13 generations), the fact that Matthew divides the genealogy like this is significant. The calling of Abraham, the kingdom of David, the exile in Babylon and the coming of the Messiah are all significant events in the ongoing story of God's people. God promised Abraham that he would bless all the nations through him (Genesis 12:1–3). God covenanted with David to bless his line and the people (e.g. Psalm 89:19–37). The exile in Babylon was a wake-up call to God's people to live in holiness or God would punish them. The Messiah came to renew the relationship between God and his people.

The genealogy also reveals something of our identity. Many Jews hoped for a new era of peace and justice, in which foreign political domination was ended, the poor were no longer oppressed, the land was fruitful and people were healed of sickness. Some of them expected this era to be ushered in by a messiah, or perhaps two messiahs. (Ancient Jewish texts give different pictures. The Psalms of Solomon 17—18 speak of one royal messiah. The Testaments of the Twelve Patriarchs and some Dead Sea scrolls speak of two messiahs, one royal and one priestly.) The messiah would come to save God's people and bring peace to the nations, to fulfil the promise to Abraham that God's people would bring blessing to all peoples. Jesus is our Messiah and so brings us into this people of blessing. As we now belong to this story of salvation, we are called to be the people through whom God brings his blessing to all peoples.

2 Focus on Joseph

Matthew 1:18–25

We tend to focus on Jesus and the fulfilment of prophecies when we read this text, but the story's main actor is actually Joseph. Despite the fact that he is introduced in verse 18 and from there remains the key focus of the action through to verse 25, we sideline him to focus on Jesus and Mary. We often think through how the annunciation and subsequent pregnancy affected Mary, but what about Joseph?

Honour and shame were part and parcel of everyday life. Mary's pregnancy would only have brought shame on Joseph: shame if people thought he was the father and shame if they thought the father was someone else. Joseph was about to suffer the humiliation of people diminishing his masculinity and sexuality, which is destructive for any man. His only chance of reclaiming some honour publicly would be to heap the humiliation on her. But Joseph does not. Until the angel informs him of the reality of the situation, he decides to resolve the situation in the way that causes least shame for her. He does this because he is righteous (v. 19). Righteousness is a key theme for Matthew, and here he gives us a picture of what it looks like: putting the other first even when we face personally destructive situations.

Joseph also shows quite extraordinary self-control and self-sacrifice. He had no sex with his wife for the first part, possibly nine months, of his married life (vv. 24–25). He seems to have done so in obedience to God. The angel told him that Mary was fulfilling the prophecy 'a *virgin* will conceive and give birth to a son', that is, a virgin would give birth as well as conceive. Joseph did as the angel commanded: 'he took Mary as his wife *and* did not have sex with her until she bore a son'. Most men would find this quite challenging. Costly obedience is another key theme in Matthew that he introduces through Joseph.

Joseph also acts obediently in naming their son Jesus (vv. 21, 25). Interestingly, this is to fulfil a prophecy in which the baby boy will be named Emmanuel (v. 23). Matthew has no concerns about identifying these two clearly different names. He does so to say something about the character of God – 'God is with us' is God saving us from our sins, bringing us into righteousness and obedience.

3 Acting like the people of God

Matthew introduces Jesus' birth in terms of its location and the reign in which it took place. Both are significant, not least in terms of Jesus being God with his people and saving them from their sins. Jesus was born 'in Bethlehem in Judea' (v. 1), fulfilling the prophecy that a leader would come from there who would shepherd God's people Israel (v. 6). Shepherding God's people was the role of the king of Israel and involved wisely governing the nation that all might prosper and live in justice and peace. The prophets noted that many kings failed in this task, but God would raise up a good shepherd from David's line (e.g. Ezekiel 34). By virtue of Joseph being a son of David (1:16, 20) and married to Mary, Matthew attaches Jesus to the royal line of David and, with the place of his birth, he announces that Jesus is the great ruler who will shepherd Israel. He is, as the Magi put it, the 'king of the Jews' (v. 2).

This brings him into conflict with Herod, whom Matthew only calls 'King' (v. 1) – not, interestingly, the 'king of the Jews'. Herod was Idumean, not Jewish, and became king over Judea through partnership with the Roman Empire. He was notorious for his deep insecurity, which led him to kill even members of his family. The reactions we see in this passage are typical. Matthew intimates that his interest in finding Jesus has nothing to do with worship, but securing his power base, as we see later in the chapter. Herod plots to kill Jesus secretly (v. 7), just as Joseph had planned to save Mary from disgrace secretly (1:19); his selfishness and murderous intent stand in stark contrast to Joseph's righteousness. We see in Herod a very different kind of man.

All of this begs a question: if Herod, all Jerusalem, the chief priests and the scribes of the people are inveigled in some way in Herod's plan to kill Jesus, how does Jesus save his people from their sins? The Gentile Magi look much more like Jesus' people, not least as they fall down and worship him (v. 11). Through this contrast Matthew introduces another theme: who really are Jesus' people – the ones who say they are or the ones who act like it?

4 Faithfulness to God and God's own faithfulness

Matthew 2:13–15

Matthew focuses on Joseph again. Just as in the previous Joseph story (1:18–25), an angel of the Lord appears to Joseph in a dream, commands him to take a particular course of action and Joseph obediently carries out the instruction. To underline Joseph's obedience, Matthew uses almost exactly the same Greek words to describe both the angelic order and Joseph's actions (translated: 'Get up, take the child and his mother and *flee* to Egypt and be there until' [v. 13] and 'he got up, took the child and his mother *by night* and *went away* to Egypt' [vv. 14–15] – the words in italics are those not repeated). Joseph continues to model the life of righteousness to which Jesus will call people later in the gospel.

The similarity between the two Joseph stories is not accidental. These two stories surround the first Herod story and serve to highlight the key difference between Joseph and Herod. (The technique of surrounding one story with two linked stories was well known to biblical writers.) Joseph seeks to be righteous, even when this might damage himself. He listens to the word of the Lord through the angel, and he obeys it. Herod seeks to discern the guidance of God to the Magi in order to serve himself and thwart (if this were possible) the purposes of God.

For Matthew, this is all deeply ironic. As a result of Herod trying to thwart the plans of God, God commands Joseph to take the child and his mother to Egypt from where they will come back some day. This means that Jesus will fulfil again the ancient prophecy, 'out of Egypt I have called my son' (Hosea 11:1). Just as Hosea had spoken of the Hebrews being called by God out of slavery in Egypt, so Matthew saw Jesus the Messiah and Son of God coming out of Egypt. Just as the exodus brought salvation in the promised land, so Jesus will bring salvation from sin and death. It is as if Matthew wants to remind us of another Joseph who had dreams, also went to Egypt in difficult circumstances and was able later to testify that what others had done for evil, God had used for good.

5 Holding to God's promise in tragedy

The story moves back to Herod. Furious that the wise men have tricked him, he orders the murder of all the children in Bethlehem and the surrounding areas. Estimates suggest that the population of the region was probably under 1,000. This means that roughly 20 baby boys would have been killed by those Herod sent to do this task. This was typical behaviour for Herod the Great. He had many members of the royal household eliminated along with their supporters, including his favourite wife Mariamne and his three eldest sons. He even laid plans for the slaughter of the Jewish nobility on his death so that people really would be mourning during his funeral (even though they would most likely be mourning for others rather than for him). His desire to cling to the throne against the will of God plunged him and others into tragedy.

Even here, Matthew sees hope. With a certain tenderness, he cites a verse from Jeremiah which pictures weeping and mourning. Jewish children had been lost in the military campaign by either the Assyrian or Babylonian armies in the eighth or sixth century BC (scholarly opinion is divided). Either way, Jacob's wife, the matriarch Rachel, is pictured as mourning for her children, that is, the children of Israel or Judah. The words Matthew cites end with the image of this mother mourning and refusing to be comforted because her children have been taken away and will never return to her. Leaving the story with this image, Matthew makes us acknowledge human tragedy and grief.

Despite the fact that his storytelling technique will not allow us to move glibly from genuine loss to any triumph won by Christ, Matthew sounds an underlying note of hope. The verses in Jeremiah which follow immediately from the one Matthew cites (Jeremiah 31:16–17) offer Rachel hope beyond her grief with the promise that her children will come out of exile and back to their own country. The very next story (Matthew 2:19–23) has Jesus come back from his temporary exile in Egypt to Palestine. While Matthew will not allow us to move too hastily from tragedy and loss, he does not let go of the hope that God will fulfil his promise – a lesson in lament.

6 Challenging obedience

The prophecy fulfilled in this section, 'he will be called a Nazarene' (v. 23), has caused much discussion. It occurs nowhere in the Old Testament. Some suggest that Isaiah 4:3 has been changed from 'he shall be called holy' to 'he shall be called a Nazirite' (on such holy people, see Numbers 6:1–21) and then to 'he shall be called a Nazarene' (using wordplay on Nazirite and Nazarene). Others suggest that the messianic prophecy in Isaiah 11:1 is in view: 'a shoot will come forth from the stump of Jesse, a branch [Hebrew *netzer*] will grow out of his roots.' None of the many explanations has won general consent among scholars, largely because they are all quite convoluted. Possibly the prophecy has been lost from the Old Testament in the same way that Jesus' words 'It is more blessed to give than to receive' (Acts 20:35) can be found nowhere in the gospels.

What can be known from the text is that Joseph continues to model the obedience of the righteous believer in God. His young family has escaped Herod's slaughter and is settled in Egypt. But just as God called Moses from his settled life in Midian back to the danger of Egypt, so he calls Joseph back to Israel. Joseph obeys and again Matthew underlines his obedience by using almost exactly the same words to describe Joseph's response to the angel (v. 21) as he did in quoting the angel's instruction (v. 20). Joseph puts not only his but his family's life on the line to obey God. We hear the faintest echo of the story of Abraham and Isaac in Genesis 22.

However, God is aware of and compassionate towards Joseph. Returning to Israel, Joseph is uneasy as Herod's son Archelaus is ruling Judea. Joseph was right to be wary, as Archelaus ordered the massacre of 3,000 Jews who were fomenting a rebellion at a Passover festival soon after his father's death. God responds to Joseph's concerns. An angel warns Joseph in another dream and he takes his family up to Galilee, where they set up home in Nazareth. Whatever the origin of the prophecy 'he will be called a Nazarene', Matthew claims that this move fulfils it – interestingly, not that Jesus *actually was* one, for Matthew has already shown that he was from Bethlehem in accordance with the prophecy of Micah.

Guidelines

We all have a story, but none of us wanders through our own narrative in isolation. Stories mingle and intertwine; our stories affect others' stories and theirs affect ours. Matthew's birth narrative intermingles the stories of three men: Jesus, Herod and Joseph. (Mary takes the lead role in Luke's birth narrative, but that honour goes to Joseph in Matthew's account.) Joseph opens the series of five stories, plays lead actor in the first, third and last, and his actions close the account.

Like an innocent bystander who gets caught up in the action of a thriller, Joseph unwittingly finds himself at the centre of political intrigue and a murderous plot, and he has to flee abroad for his life – and all because of a baby that he has not fathered. As the action opens, Joseph is engaged to Mary. He is a handyman. Suddenly, Joseph's fiancée is pregnant, he is having angelic visions and receiving VIP visitors, the king is trying to kill their baby boy and he becomes a refugee to protect his family.

Why was all this happening? Because his life had become inextricably intertwined with that of the baby Jesus. Living with Jesus will bring changes to our lives. Pause to reflect on what differences Jesus has already made to your life and what new challenges he may be calling you to. Take some time to pray through these things, giving thanks for what he has done already and asking his help for the new things he would do in and through you.

None of this was easy for Joseph. He was called to obey when his masculinity and sexuality were diminished and so much of his identity as a man was threatened, to obey when his family's lives were threatened, to obey in such a way that meant he gave up his job, home and all financial security, and then to give it all up again when called back to a still dangerous homeland. Joseph models the obedient believer Jesus calls each one of us to be later in this gospel. How will we respond to Jesus' call to a life of radical obedience to his teaching?

FURTHER READING

W.D. Davies and Dale C. Allison, *A Critical and Exegetical Commentary on the Gospel according to Saint Matthew* (T&T Clark, 2004).

R.T. France, *The Gospel of Matthew* (Eerdmans, 2007).

Daniel J. Harrington, *Sacra Pagina: The gospel of Matthew* (The Liturgical Press, 1991).

Ageing and family relations

Harriet and Donald Mowat

We are all ageing. Average life expectancy in the UK has recently risen to 80 for women and 75 for men, with 30% of the UK population now being over 60. Despite the seductions of a variety of pills, potions and procedures that claim to stave off the much-feared 'appearances' of ageing, we will all age until we die.

We will all be affected by the ageing demographic: some of us will have to work longer, postponing retirement; some will become carers for ageing relatives; and some will take up a career in elder care as demand increases. Some of us will fall ill with typical age-related illnesses of stroke, heart disease, osteoporosis, dementia and depression. As we age, we will inevitably focus on our health; for many, maintaining independence will be our priority.

Many in their midlife find themselves living between their care for grandchildren and the needs of older relatives, friends or neighbours. Longer lives mean more generations coexisting; complex caring relationships evolve alongside the decline in the 'traditional' nuclear family. One way or another, our church communities reflect these changes.

For these next two weeks, we will look at how we, as Christian people, might approach and rejoice in ageing. How can we age as well as possible and support others, often our family, to do the same?

In the first week, we think about what we might mean by ageing, by family relationships. In the second week, we focus on how we can use faith as a guide for our ageing journey. The biblical passages we have chosen are wide-ranging and offer opportunity for some insights. Age is presented in the scriptures as both a blessing and a curse, an opportunity for growth, change and surprises as well as inevitable limitations. Families are central to the social structure described in the scriptures, as they are today. They can be units of safety or discomfort. Relationships have to be negotiated. How can your faith grow as a result of your life experience as you age?

Unless otherwise stated, Bible quotations are from the New Revised Standard Version (Anglicised).

1 For everything there is a season

Ecclesiastes 3:1–8; 12:1–7

These two well-known passages from Ecclesiastes set the scene of the trajectory of life and its circularity. Ageing is part of the life cycle. The passages provide contrasting moods of light and dark, hope and despair, love and hate, building up and breaking down. The first passage gives us stark polarities within which we are all required to navigate. These readings give us a map. Life is difficult and ageing is part of life, but life can also be full of hope and joy. Setting our compass of faith as soon as we can helps us through some its vicissitudes. In the second reading, the advice is to learn about our creator early on, to find our bearings and to create an unbreakable attachment. Feeling securely attached to God, feeling loved and loving God will help us when things get challenging. Being grounded in a growing faith helps us through some of the tough times.

Tradition looks to aged people for story and for context. Elders can reassure and confirm that there is 'nothing new under the sun' (Ecclesiastes 1:9). Elders provide, through their own experiences, a sense of continuity. The commandments bid us to love one another and to honour our fathers and mothers – our older folk. Elders, despite being utterly capable of dishonour and folly, should be heard and respected. The hope is that older people will be more balanced, sensible and just than their youthful selves; that ageing is an opportunity for development and growth; that older people will improve themselves as they age.

Ageing provides a hope for us, that we can change and become better people through reflection on our life experience. A proper concept of ageing also acknowledges the way in which our inevitable human frailties persist despite our search for virtues, best intentions and length of years. Older people are ordinary, flawed people. We are all ageing.

2 Ageing is a spiritual journey

Matthew 18:1–7; 1 Corinthians 13:11–13

Sometimes we can be our own worst enemies or our own stumbling blocks. In this passage from Matthew, Jesus responds to the childish questions of his disciples about who is the greatest. He calls a child to him and tells his disciples that they must be like the child. They must be childlike, rather than childish, in order to get into heaven; they must change. Walking with God and growing in faith involve retaining a childlike interest and wonder in the world.

As we 'grow up', we put together our knowledge and get better at understanding the world, its structures, its institutions and the way in which people operate. We learn how things actually work, and we move away from the intuitive knowledge we had as a child. Ageing offers us the opportunity not only to grow in wisdom, to make changes, but also to reacquire childlike knowledge. Sometimes we find what we learn to be too difficult or distasteful to accept, and so we provide stumbling blocks to our learning. We resist change. Jesus exhorts us to change – ageing is a process of change. Carl Jung famously tells us that 'we cannot live the afternoon of life according to the programme of life's morning. For what was great in the morning will be little in the evening and what in the morning was true will at evening have become a lie' (*Collected Works Vol. 8: Structure and dynamics of the psyche* , 1969, p. 399).

In 1 Corinthians, we learn from this very familiar passage that as we develop we must put an end to childish things; we can no longer be naive and innocent of the difficulties of life, but we must be, we suggest, childlike in our absorption of new information and sustenance of hope.

It is easy for faith, hope and love, those qualities of the child, to be extinguished as we experience the world. As we grow up, we can become subject to the temptation of meaninglessness. We can become overwhelmed by the material over the spiritual. One of our ageing tasks and duties is to remain hopeful for ourselves and others and to remember that ageing is a spiritual matter.

3 Ageing can be fearsome

Psalm 71:17–24; 39:4–8

In western societies, we are strongly influenced by a linear image of ageing, which suggests a curve of *achievement*. Ageing is portrayed as a process of development and then decline. This is illustrated in Shakespeare's famous 'stages of man' soliloquy, delivered by Jaques in *As You Like It*: when we move from infancy to old age and are 'sans everything'. Our default image of ageing is increasing decrepitude. This is evident in the general tone attached to ageing in Psalms and Proverbs. No wonder we fear and deny age. However, as we move through the centuries, we are slowly discovering the extraordinary complexity and wonder of the human body and mind and its possibilities. We are all part of this journey of discovery. Our ageing journeys are less formulaic than we have hitherto understood.

These two passages from Psalms 71 and 39 give a flavour of some of the common worries and concerns about ageing. We learn as we age that life seems suddenly, in retrospect, rather short, just a few hand breadths, and sometimes quite difficult. There is a danger that we feel abandoned. We are uncertain as to what is to happen next to us. Can our individual lives be that important to God? This echoes the passage we have already read in Ecclesiastes. There is a certain turmoil expressed in these passages, fear of being treated as idiots. We fear that our lives are meaningless. We fear dying unforgiven.

Any possible hope and meaning are to be found in God's constancy and protective capacity, and in the extraordinary possibilities of positive relationships one with another. That is what we wait for. God is our teacher. In Psalm 71, the psalmist clearly has recognised himself as ageing, noting his grey hair, but sees proclaiming the righteousness of God as part of his ageing task. Faith and creativity give comfort in old age. Singing and music in this passage are important parts of experiencing God. Through singing and playing music, we can tell the story of God; the story of God is our own story.

4 What is family?

Mark 3:31–34; Matthew 8:18–22; John 19:25–27

The gospels give us much to contemplate as to what might constitute family. On the one hand, much is made of lineage – who is related to whom and so on – but, on the other hand, Jesus is quite dismissive of family taking any special place in his affections or practices. 'Who are my mother and my brothers?' he asks (Mark 3:33), irritated by the distraction from his teaching ministry. He later hands over the care of his mother to his beloved friend at the foot of the cross (John 19:26). He asks us to prioritise, making it difficult for people to follow him and to attend to family responsibilities at the same time: 'Let the dead bury their own dead' (Matthew 8:22). None of this sits easily with the romanticised view of family, which implies close loving relationships.

Families are complex and dynamic social structures, reflecting the psychological complexity of attachments in human relationships. Old Testament ideas of family are dominated by lineage, heritage and the binding together through property, including women. Vestiges of this persist today. Family can be the name given to a group of biologically unrelated people who nevertheless see themselves as responsible for the welfare of each other, such as a church community. Increasing numbers of single older people living alone challenge our conventional ideas of family; care home managers often speak about their residents as being a 'kind of family'. Families can bring light and love and support, and families can harbour darkness, despair and cruelty.

Duties of care bound up in the understanding of family have to be thought about quite carefully. Health and social welfare systems in the UK are predicated on the assumption of a narrow version of a nuclear family, which implies a duty of care even when there is no emotional warmth and indeed sometimes outright hostility.

Jesus has some difficult things to say about families. He makes clear a need to scrutinise hitherto unquestioned duty when he suggests to the young man intending to bury his father before following him that he has his priorities wrong. To prioritise the burial would be to behave as if nothing had changed in the meeting of Jesus. 'Carry on being dead if you want to,' is the clear message. Jesus suggests that attention is best paid to what is in front of us, rather than blindly adhering to family or societal expectations and traditions. Family traditions unthinkingly handed down may become a stumbling block for the next generation.

5 Leaving family: changing families

Psalm 128; Matthew 10:16–22; 10:34–40

Psalm 128 is a lovely short psalm that affirms in an idealistic way the benign and supportive structure of family life as portrayed in the Old Testament. Here we have secure attachment within the family and its linear continuity, which offers prosperity, peace and plenty. There are children and grand-children to be enjoyed and nurtured, and the wife is at the centre of the structure like the vine. This shows the centrality of the nurturing feminine, represented as growth and fruitfulness. Children are like olive shoots. Families are reinforced and supported. This all comes as a consequence of 'fearing' and loving the Lord and walking in his ways. There will be peace and happiness and blessings for those who love God. Here is an unprob-lematic family structure, one that is still held up as the ideal aspiration by many of us, and that is certainly enshrined in our social and health care policy assumptions.

However, the cosiness of this ideal of family life is somewhat blown apart in the New Testament. The arrival of Jesus heralds a change in the way we are asked to understand families. Matthew's account of what Jesus says about families is not particularly reassuring, even allowing for the under-standing that Jesus was referring to the rejection of Christian Jews by their families. Loving God and walking in his ways seems to involve leaving fami-lies and falling out with siblings and parents. This is a very different picture of family: a place of distrust, even violence and hatred.

Sometimes, leaving family is essential for spiritual growth. We need to understand our own families and constantly rework the idea of the family as things change.

Healthy functional families, however they are formed and develop, have to be places where each of us can grow spiritually, care and be cared for, and contribute to the general well-being. This should be the case at any age.

Jesus tells us to prioritise faith and belief over family, warning us that this will be a serious challenge. As we age and inevitably become more dependent, this can become ever more difficult.

6 Expectations of relationships in families

1 Timothy 5:1–18

Scriptural advice is rarely specifically age-related, but this passage gives us something to think about in terms of elder care. How should we care for one another across the generations, either in kinship families or the Christian community?

First, we should try to encourage respectful relationships between generations, particularly among fathers, sons, mothers and daughters. We should eschew harsh speech. We now live in times when there are both opportunities for and barriers to intergenerational relationships. Recent voting patterns suggest that the young and old are far apart in their thinking about society and its values. The detail of this is a little more complicated. Learning to listen to each other across the generations seems to be the essence of good relationships. Listening to stories and interpreting for each other helps ensure that respect is fostered.

Second, Paul tells us that there is a familial duty to care for those respectable older family members, those 'well attested for [their] good works' (v. 10). He particularly focuses on widows. These elders are deserving, whereas some are not. Providing for one's relatives is part of the good works and expectations of the community. But what about older people who are undeserving, who have not carried out good works? Or older people who are not part of a recognisable family?

We know that young people leave their families and create their own units. The church is also subject to that process. Young people leave church and seek spiritual answers elsewhere. In later life, they often return as people who are seeking to make sense of their world, which will have unfolded in unexpected and sometimes difficult ways. If we are wise, we will embrace older people as core church members and take more time to sustain the older people who remain in the church 'family'. Like the family members who do not care for their elderly folk, so the church that does not care for its elders is denying its faith and is in danger of succumbing to the agendas of the secular world. People, particularly those in the third age, are looking for spiritual sustenance and are searching for meaning and purpose. Are our churches willing and able to respond to this?

Guidelines

This first week, we have focused on the journey of ageing and how it is an opportunity to deepen our faith and walk closer with God. We all age; however, this common, universal experience is also unique to each of us. There is a time for everything, and we experience our lives as a process of choices and stages. Many of us are fearful of ageing and its implied decline and limitations. We have suggested that the ability to change and develop as we age is crucial to our well-being and to our ability to remain in loving relationships with whoever our family might be. We have suggested that the tasks of ageing include finding creative ways to continue to experience God's love and faithfulness to us, in particular music, dancing and singing. We have raised the difficult issues of family relationships and suggested that our traditional ideas of family sometimes need examination and thought. These are some questions that might help you reflect on some of these issues.

- How is my faith growing as a result of my life experience as I age?
- Do I feel grounded in a secure attachment to God?
- What childlike interest can I cultivate today to add to my life's wisdom?
- Are there any attitudes or practices that I need to change to invest in my ageing process?
- Who is my family?
- Where do I look for a family?
- What responsibilities do I have to my family?
- How do I care for the elders around me?
- Do I have fears about who will care for me in my old age?

30 December–5 January

1 Intergenerational concerns and care

Ruth 1:1–22; 4:13–17

In our ageing population, the responsibilities and complexities of intergenerational care increase. Health and social care services cannot manage the volume of age-related need. Families of different kinds fill the gaps. In a kin family, daughters or daughters-in-law are often the first port of call when help is needed.

The story of Ruth and Naomi is an eternal story of negotiated responsibility between family members and the sometimes surprising love that falls out of that. The relationship between Naomi and her daughters-in-law is obviously a loving one, with healthy attachment on either side. When Naomi decides to return to her own land following multiple bereavement, the daughters-in-law dutifully go with her. Despite her bereavement, Naomi manages to summon up enough courage to suggest that the daughters-in-law should not do this. She suggests instead that they go back to their mothers and find husbands from their native land. Naomi laments that she cannot provide them with husbands – she is too old. Her main role is over. Ruth famously demurs and says she will stay with her mother-in-law.

Naomi is full of both gratitude to the dear daughter-in-law Ruth and resentment about her situation. 'Call me no longer Naomi [meaning 'pleasant'], call me Mara [meaning 'bitter'],' she says to her village folk as she returns (1:20). She is trying to make the adjustments to her ageing situation. Naomi is both proud and sad, lonely and yet loved, questioning God and yet faithful.

Later, we see that Naomi wisely and subtly guides Ruth into a secure situation of marriage. Ruth and Naomi trust each other. Naomi uses her elder status and her knowledge of her extended family to make suggestions to Ruth as to how best to behave in this foreign land. Ruth finds love with Boaz, and Naomi finds that she has the care of a grandson, who goes on to himself have a grandson of great importance.

Negotiating our needs for care in old age within a family is a two-way process. Elders have a duty and responsibility to try to understand the pressures on younger people, who may want to help but will have multiple calls on their time.

2 Ageing brings change and loss

John 21:9–23

The context of this reading is a meeting post-resurrection between Simon Peter and Jesus. Peter and another disciple have been on a fishing trip. The disciples have gone back to the work that they had been engaged in before they had been called by Jesus. They have slipped back into their old familiar ways of being, perhaps not knowing what else to do. Jesus helps them haul in a huge catch – he continues to feed them. The key instruction that

Jesus gives them in this encounter is to follow him and to nourish, feed and tend others. None of the disciples dare ask him who he is because they know the answer. They are reluctant to really acknowledge that things have changed and that they needed to change.

The journey into old age is sometimes expressed in two parts: the third age, in which we can thrive and grow following the liberation and opportunities of retirement, and the fourth age, when we are struggling with normal activities of daily living. Increasingly in the UK, we will live to the fourth age. This means we will experience loss of capacity and independence. Most of us don't want to acknowledge this, even though we know it to be true. Jesus tells us in this passage that we need to do things differently once we have realised who he is. It's no use pretending it isn't going to happen.

Jesus tells Peter that he will have a difficult old age (v. 18). He will have to do things he doesn't want to do, will be unable to do the things he does want to do, and will not be able to have control over where he is taken or what is done to him. This doesn't sound at all appealing. It does sound like the fourth age.

The manner of our ageing and death is unknown to us in advance and will be different for each of us. There is certainly loss as we journey through old age, but Jesus remains the same, ever-present if we care to see him. When Peter asks about the 'other' disciple and his destiny, Jesus makes it clear that we each have to deal with our own ageing and death.

3 Be confident in your ageing

2 Timothy 4:6–8; 1 Peter 5:1–11

In her novel *A Spool of Blue Thread* (Alfred A. Knopf, 2015), Anne Tyler gives voice through her ageing characters to the difficulties and challenges expressed in a wish to be independent. One elderly woman claims to be too independent for a retirement community; her equally elderly friend replies, 'Independent? Bosh. That's just another word for selfish. It's stiff-backed people like you who end up being the biggest burdens' (p. 133).

These two biblical passages give us assurances that it is all right to be old, and that we should fear neither old age nor death. Instead, we should try to prepare ourselves through our faith. This puts us in mind of the lifetime acquisition of virtue, seen as central in the 20th century by psychoanalyst Erik Erikson, but also by many others, going back to the ancient Greeks.

Stiff-backed people are self-centred, whereas the truly free are humble, disciplined and mindful of their ageing trajectory.

We can pick up the theme from yesterday, when Jesus exhorts his disciples to follow him by tending and caring for his flock. This is a primary task for the wise older person; sometimes the emphasis on youth policy overshadows the obvious role of the older member of the church as 'stable shepherd'. It is certainly the case that most voluntary activities provided by the church are managed by older people, even if they are aimed at the young.

It can be hard work being an elder, and it is important to draw on our faith. There is a temptation to succumb in old age to doubt, and to rail against the inevitable degree of suffering. A popular birthday card depicting a decrepit older person sitting with drink in hand has a speech bubble saying, 'I can't decide whether to be a good example or a terrible warning!' This makes us laugh at the sheer difficulty of living by example.

But we need to be good examples. We aim by reflective practice to age with confidence, and to be able graciously to acknowledge the changes within us; the next generation are encouraged to learn from our own ageing practice. We particularly need good negotiating skills, so that we can maintain our sense of self, despite a need for more care, without turning our unique sense of self into a burden for others.

4 Ageing as a hopeful presence for others

Luke 2:21–38

In this well-known story, we see the baby Jesus being presented to the Lord in the temple, as all firstborn sons were. Simeon, now very old, was clearly seen as a holy man, full of the Holy Spirit and much respected for this. Simeon believed and hoped that he would one day see the salvation of Israel. This had been promised him by the Lord, and he believed this despite a lifetime of waiting.

In comes Mary with her tiny baby, no doubt worn out, along with Joseph, a man perhaps still uncertain about the events surrounding Jesus' birth, perhaps both confused and distressed. The couple hand the baby to Simeon, who miraculously recognises Jesus as the saviour of Israel and even of the world. Simeon reassures and amazes Mary and Joseph at the same time. He provides them with deep comfort. Simeon has been looking forward and hoping for this day for a long time; he has not been looking backwards with regret, but is still looking for transformation. And here it is, in the shape of a small newborn. Simeon recognises the potential. He can see the truth when it presents itself; he consoles the parents and warns them not to expect an easy ride. He confirms that his own work is now done, and he is ready to depart. He is awake to the new possibilities that salvation can bring.

Anna, who is also very old and has been a widow for years, has lived in the temple prophesying and praying since the much earlier death of her husband. She has spent a lifetime developing her faith and trying to live well.

We see confirmation of the possibilities of faith in these two old people. A large part of their ministries in older age was to pray for others. This doesn't mean that younger people cannot have great faith and great gifts, but the perseverance in faith illustrated by these two individuals is striking, and offers us a way of being in old age, particularly as we are all more likely than ever to live into our 80s and 90s, with the associated frailty and decline. Anna and Simeon epitomise the acceptance of waiting patiently and hopefully for what is promised and of looking forward with anticipation rather than dread.

5 Ageing and deepening faith

Genesis 18:1–15; Romans 4:13–22

There is an old saying: 'If you want to make God laugh, tell him your plans!' In the first of these readings, God makes Sarah laugh, but in the end has the last laugh himself. These passages confirm the salience of faith, as we contemplate ourselves in old age. The ageing journey is about faith and surprises; this week, we have been surprised by Sarah's conception and delivery of a child in very old age, and by the arrival of Naomi's grandson despite the unlikely circumstances preceding it.

In the Old Testament reading, we see that Sarah really can't take seriously the idea of conception after menopause. She laughs quietly to herself as she hears the three men talking about lineage. However, they challenge her conventional wisdom about her barren status and, in the right season, she does indeed bear a child. Abraham does therefore become the father of all nations. So we should be careful of assumptions about old age: God had other plans for Sarah and Abraham. The word of God comes to us through different media. Sarah represents the conventional response to the idea of wonder in old age; conventional thinking, along tramlines, can reduce and dampen our faith.

Despite our ageing bodies – being 'as good as dead' – we are wise to be alive to the word of God, which is often received and given through hospitality. Sarah is busy making cakes for the visitors and preparing a meal. It is during this process that she is told of her next steps.

In his letter to the Romans, Paul seems to be suggesting that the law, and the social norms and stereotypes enshrined within it, are not to be taken too literally if we are to expand our horizons of faith. The law shuts things down and constricts; the social conventions and stereotypes of old age that currently prevail are that older people are mostly a nuisance, unproductive and likely to be a drain on resources. Older people are required to fit into what is expected of them. There is a tension between the law as found in institutional regulations, practices and provision on the one hand, and the expression of self and faith in the individual on the other. Managing that tension is part of the struggle to find our full creativity in older age.

6 Finding meaning and purpose in later life

Hebrews 11:1–22

One of the tasks of ageing, and a task by default of those caring for older people, is to help people to find and confirm meaning and purpose to life, as these lives draw towards their endings. In this compelling passage in the letter to the Hebrews, we are given the means of doing this: 'Have faith, lead lives through faith and be guided by faith', rather than by what is happening in the world.

We are encouraged to see ourselves as threads in a tapestry, in a direct connection with our ancestors, as opposed to thinking in terms of our specific individual and worldly existences. As we grow older, our vision needs to change from the immediate concern and preoccupation with worldly things to those things that are not visible but in whose existence we have faith. This is a hard task, given that we live in societies where who we are and what we do (or have done) very much defines our future place and worth. This passage from Hebrews suggests that the reality is otherwise. It is the spiritual trajectory that is the meaningful one. The spirit doesn't die, but instead we all contribute to the continuing greater creation through our spirits and creativity. Our spiritual focus helps us overcome and bear the suffering of life, with its inevitable trials and tribulations. Hebrews 11 conveys these spiritual issues by giving examples from those prominent in the Judeo-Christian story. Such a spiritual search applies to each one of us throughout life, but in old age it seems we are particularly in need of a spiritual focus.

We don't know what the future holds. We learn from our forefathers that persisting in faith and believing in God's promises, despite the immediate and sometimes contrary worldly pressures, pay off in the end. It is not for us to know our place or our end; indeed, it is in our very 'not knowing' that our faith develops.

Finally, this passage reminds us of our Judeo-Christian heritage and our hopes for peaceful reconciliation one with another and with God. Our ageing will inevitably make us vulnerable, but it will also afford us the opportunity to pursue our faith and spiritual lives. As older people, we are encouraged to do this; we can in turn encourage the younger generation through our actions and practices.

Guidelines

This second week, we have concentrated on the way in which our faith can help us age and guide us through the tribulations that will surely come. We have thought about intergenerational concerns, and how youth and age can help each other to maintain hope and meaning, as Ruth and Naomi did. We acknowledge that ageing, while bringing loss and change, can also be an opportunity for deepening our faith and finding meaning and purpose in our lives. Faith can help us to be confident and steadfast about our ageing and keep us alert for surprises along the way. As we age, we have a continuing yet changed place in the world. One of our roles as older people is to be a hopeful presence for others by showing a constancy of faith and hope. We hope that these questions will help you consider these issues. You might want to take two or three of these questions and discuss them with your family and friends, and think about changes you might be able to make in the light of these discussions.

- As I approach older age, what are the things that might make be bitter?
- Who is lovingly there for me in the difficult times?
- What losses am I beginning to experience?

- How can I learn to adjust to the changes ageing is bringing, trusting in the strength that Jesus provides in my life?
- What are the things I can still do to care for others?
- What moments of recognition of the holy have I experienced throughout my life?
- What light am I still waiting for?
- Who do I need to pray for, for that light to enter their lives?
- How do I keep my mind open to the surprises life still wants to bring me?
- What are the spiritual practices that continue to sustain me and deepen my faith?
- How do I see my life in the context of faithful obedience?

FURTHER READING

Joan Chittister, *The Gift of Years: Growing older gracefully* (Darton, Longman and Todd, 2008).

Emilie Griffin, *Souls in Full Sail: A Christian spirituality for the later years* (IVP Books, 2011).

Malcolm Johnson and Joanna Walker, *Spiritual Dimension of Ageing* (Cambridge University Press, 2016).

Frits de Lange, *Loving Later Life: An ethics of ageing* (Eerdmans, 2015).

Harriet Mowat and Donald Mowat, *The Freedom of Years: Ageing in perspective* (BRF, 2018).

M. Scott Peck, *The Road Less Travelled* (Simon Schuster, 2001).

Richard Rohr, *Falling Upward: A spirituality for the two halves of life* (Jossey Bass, 2011).

John Swinton, *Dementia: Living in the memories of God* (Eerdmans, 2012).

James Woodward, *Valuing Age: Pastoral ministry with older people* (SPCK, 2008).

Overleaf... Guidelines forthcoming issue | Author profile |
Recommended reading | Order and subscription forms

Guidelines forthcoming issue

HELEN PAYNTER

This edition of *Guidelines* marks the transition period between two commissioning editors. David Spriggs is retiring after many years of distinguished service, and I am taking over this role, although you will be reading work that David commissioned for some months to come. So it is with a feeling of excitement that I have been reviewing the submissions for the next edition; it is rather like opening a parcel that someone else has ordered for me!

Some of the writers are already familiar to me. I had the privilege of sitting under Ernest Lucas' teaching at Bristol Baptist College, and so I had high expectations of what he might be offering. I was not disappointed; his perceptive studies on characters within Proverbs and some of the key themes in the book are rich fare. Similarly I am acquainted with Nigel Wright's work through a number of his books, and I am confident that we will all be challenged in Lent by his notes on 'the way of the cross'.

Other writers are new to me. Pauline Hoggarth's helpful reflections on the first half of Jeremiah are in this volume, and she will be completing our study of Jeremiah next time, with readings that include the challenging question of the impact of trauma and suffering on our spiritual growth. Andy Angel has already given us a thought-provoking set of studies on Matthew's birth and infancy narratives. Next time he will continue our journey through Matthew with three weeks of readings on chapters 3—7.

Leading up to Easter, we have a week of reflections on Holy Week from David Spriggs, who will look at the seven words from the cross. I always feel I am on holy ground when I listen to Jesus' dying words, and I am confident that David's contributions will lead us through that holy place most helpfully. We will then spend Easter week itself in the company of Graham Dow, who will show us, among other things, how Easter Sunday is 'the redemption of the whole created order'. Graham brings us insights that may surprise even those who have been through the Christian year many times.

Helen Morris is a new writer in the next edition of *Guidelines*. Helen did her PhD in contemporary ecclesiology and is now on the faculty at Moorlands College. She will be taking us through Paul's letter to the Ephesians, in a set of readings for the Easter season that I believe will inspire our minds and warm our hearts.

Bill Goodman will take us back to Ezekiel and will show us the growing trajectory of hope that emerges in the second half of the book. Finally, I will be offering some thoughts on the biblical concept of hospitality.

I hope I have whetted your appetite! As Ernest Lucas says in his notes on Proverbs, 'Teachability is the most frequently mentioned attribute of the wise in Proverbs. Wisdom is not just something innate. It needs to be acquired through instruction and training and this is not easy. It is an ongoing process.'

I am confident that the forthcoming issue of *Guidelines* will be useful to us as we seek to acquire wisdom.

Profile: Helen Paynter

 I consider myself blessed that God got hold of me very young. This meant that my teenage years were spent (among other things) reading the Bible through two or three times. I guess it was around this time that I was able to move from puzzlement to affirmation when I sang in church:

Lord for the word, that word of life which fires us,
speaks to our hearts and sets our souls ablaze,
teaches and trains, rebukes us and inspires us,
Lord of the word, receive your people's praise.

I went to university to study medicine, became very busy, got married, and the Bible became a bit less pressing for me. I never entirely stopped reading it, but it wasn't so important in my life, and I knew – deep down – that I was the poorer for it.

Then two things happened around the same time. After years of trying, my husband and I finally found a church that fed our souls and warmed our hearts. And a friend gave my husband a copy of the marvellous book by Gordon Fee and Douglas Stuart, *How to Read the Bible for All Its Worth*.

It was as if something had been switched on inside us both. The Spirit was rekindling our love for him, and at the same time we were learning that the Bible could be read in deeper, more challenging, more satisfying ways. These two things went absolutely hand-in-hand. There never has been, for me, a conflict between my heart worship and my head understanding.

Eventually, my path led me to Bristol Baptist College to train for ministry, and there I discovered how much more there is to reading the Bible. I learned to read for its big themes, spot how texts talk to one another, listen for the echoes of an earlier passage in a later one. I learned to use literature analysis to dig deeper into texts. And everything I learned – and continue to learn – dances in my head, plays within my mind and imagination, and enters into constant dialogue with newspapers, films and books I read and watch.

A very significant event happened for me around 2006, before I came to do any formal theological education. I received a phone call from our church youth worker asking me how she should advise a young person who had been reading some of the Old Testament stories of violence and was in danger of losing her faith because of them. Although I don't think I had anything helpful to say about them at the time, the question lodged in my mind and has since been the focus of a great deal of my research and thinking. The misuse of these texts to justify violence and the idea that these stories threaten our belief in a good God are two of the pressing issues facing the church in this generation, in my opinion. At present, I believe that one of the chief calls on my life is to try to help us address this question.

So the Bible continues to set my soul ablaze a little more with every passing year. And I'll finish by quoting from another hymn, with a little couplet that feels like one of the theme songs of my life:

The Lord has yet more light and truth
To break forth from his word.

An extract from *Image of the Invisible*

As we look towards the incarnation at Christmas, we consider how God chose to express himself, in a moment in history, as a tiny baby. But what other images describe God in the Bible, and what can we learn about his character through them? How does an invisible God reveal himself to us in scripture and in Jesus? Amy Robinson, a poet and storyteller, answers this question with imagination in BRF's Advent book for 2019.

The Bible is full of metaphors for God, images that help us to experience a little of his character. Some of them are more familiar to us than others, perhaps because of well-known verses, songs or prayers in which God is named as a rock, a good shepherd, a king.

'Metaphor', from the Greek *meta* (between) and *phero* (I carry), literally means 'carrying across'. In fact the word 'transfer' comes from exactly the same two words in Latin. So we can think of each of these biblical images as a way for our huge, inexplicable, incomprehensible God to be carried across to us, transferred from a heavenly truth to an earthly understanding. Each metaphor does this so that we can comprehend, encounter, and worship God. The rich number of images mean that we are able to keep meeting God, and praising him, in new ways throughout the seasons of our lives.

Metaphors for God respond to human need: sometimes we may greet him with joy like the morning star, at other times we may hide in him as our stronghold, run to him as our parent, feed on him as our bread. Since God is best described in relationship like this, each metaphor for God also has something to teach us about ourselves, our spiritual needs and how we can find those deep needs met in God. In every metaphor for God, we will find ourselves also pictured: as a baby bird hiding under its mother's wings, or as people who are hungry or thirsty or stranded, or as someone waiting in darkness and longing for light. The better we know God in scripture, the better we see our own spiritual condition as well.

Very early on in the western church, before the sixth century, a tradition began of singing seven Advent prayers, one for each day of the week leading up to Christmas. These are known as the 'O Antiphons', and each one addresses the coming Christ directly, using one of the titles that comes from an image in the Old Testament. The O Antiphons imaginatively link us to the people who were waiting for the first coming of Christ, needing the Messiah they had been promised. The images not only offer us metaphors for God, but for humanity without God: people in need of wisdom, a king, a key.

This book, leaning in to the tradition of the Advent antiphons, offers a selection of metaphors for God, not just for the final seven days, but for every day of Advent and all twelve days of Christmas, finishing with Epiphany on 6 January. I would like to invite you to explore them all and to pray with me, addressing God with all these different names, so that we can wonder all the more richly at the incarnation: the fact that, in Jesus, we have the 'Image of the Invisible God', God with us on earth. In Jesus, at Christmas, the waiting was over and all the needs and hopes named in the antiphons were fulfilled.

To order a copy of this book, please use the order form on page 151 or visit brfonline.org.uk.

Recommended reading

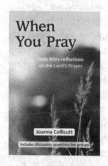

In this updated edition of a classic text, Joanna Collicutt shows how growing as a Christian is rooted in the prayer Jesus gave us. As we pray the Lord's Prayer, we express our relationship with God, absorb gospel values and are also motivated to live them out. As we pray to the Father, in union with the Son, through the power of the Spirit, so we begin to take on the character of Christ.

When You Pray
Daily Bible reflections on the Lord's Prayer
Joanna Collicutt
978 0 85746 867 3 £10.99
brfonline.org.uk

What can we learn from Augustine? There are many books that tell the life story of Augustine and how he has been fundamental in shaping western Christian theology and practice. This is not one of them. This book is about how he became a Christian – the problems he faced; the doubts he struggled with. It is about how he made sense of his belief in God, and shared it with other people. It is about how he learned to read the Bible, and to pray. And it is about the word which is at the heart of his Christian life – love. It concludes with moments of prayer from Augustine's life, in which he glimpses visions of God, encouraging the reader to take their own next steps in discipleship.

Augustine's Life of Prayer, Learning and Love
Lessons for Christian living
Cally Hammond
978 0 85746 713 3 £9.99
brfonline.org.uk

To order

Online: brfonline.org.uk
Telephone: +44 (0)1865 319700
Mon–Fri 9.15–17.30

Delivery times within the UK are
normally 15 working days. Prices are
correct at the time of going to press
but may change without prior notice.

Title	Price	Qty	Total
God of Violence Yesterday, God of Love Today?	£9.99		
Finding God in a Culture of Fear	£8.99		
BRF Advent book: Image of the Invisible	£8.99		
When You Pray	£10.99		
Augustine's Life of Prayer, Learning and Love	£9.99		

POSTAGE AND PACKING CHARGES			
Order value	UK	Europe	Rest of world
Under £7.00	£2.00	£5.00	£7.00
£7.00–£29.99	£3.00	£9.00	£15.00
£30.00 and over	FREE	£9.00 + 15% of order value	£15.00 + 20% of order value

Total value of books	
Postage and packing	
Total for this order	

Please complete in BLOCK CAPITALS

Title _____ First name/initials _____ Surname _____

Address _____

_____ Postcode _____

Acc. No. _____ Telephone _____

Email _____

Method of payment

❏ Cheque (made payable to BRF)   ❏ MasterCard / Visa

Card no. [ ][ ][ ][ ] [ ][ ][ ][ ] [ ][ ][ ][ ] [ ][ ][ ][ ]

Expires end [M][M] [Y][Y]   Security code* [ ][ ][ ]   Last 3 digits on the reverse of the card

Signature* _____ Date _____ /_____ /_____

*ESSENTIAL IN ORDER TO PROCESS YOUR ORDER

Please return this form to:
BRF, 15 The Chambers, Vineyard, Abingdon OX14 3FE | enquiries@brf.org.uk
To read our terms and find out about cancelling your order, please visit brfonline.org.uk/terms.

The Bible Reading Fellowship (BRF) is a Registered Charity (233280)

Let's build a better world

Today's children are global citizens. Modern technology means that the latest news from across the world can be broadcast in seconds, and communications with North or South America, Africa, Asia or Australasia are simply a click away.

As travel between countries becomes faster, we also tend to move around more. Many of today's children will live alongside people from other countries with different cultures, customs and beliefs. Even within Christianity itself, there can be differences in how the faith is celebrated from one country to the next.

Our Barnabas in Schools team has been exploring this theme all year with schools across England and Wales. Through 'Christianity around the World', they've taken children on a journey to learn about how faith is practised in countries such as Ethiopia, Argentina, Spain and Russia. It's all part of our aim to help the next generation grow to love and accept each other and ultimately build a better world.

How can you help? You can be part of this vision too by leaving a gift in your will to BRF. Gifts in wills help us teach Christianity creatively within the school curriculum, and every year over 20,000 children experience our Barnabas RE Days exploring 'Christianity around the World' and other themes.

Gifts in wills don't need to be huge to help us make a real difference and, for every £1 we receive, we typically invest 95p back into charitable activities.

For further information about making a gift to BRF in your will, please visit **brf.org.uk/lastingdifference**, contact us at **+44 (0)1865 319700** or email **giving@brf.org.uk**.

Whatever you can do or give, we thank you for your support.

Pray. Give. Get involved.
brf.org.uk

SHARING OUR VISION – MAKING A GIFT

I would like to make a gift to support BRF. Please use my gift for:

☐ where it is needed most ☐ Barnabas in Schools ☐ Parenting for Faith
☐ Messy Church ☐ The Gift of Years

Title	First name/initials	Surname

Address

	Postcode

Email

Telephone

Signature	Date

giftaid it   You can add an extra 25p to every £1 you give.

Please treat as Gift Aid donations all qualifying gifts of money made

☐ today, ☐ in the past four years, ☐ and in the future.

I am a UK taxpayer and understand that if I pay less Income Tax and/or Capital Gains Tax in the current tax year than the amount of Gift Aid claimed on all my donations, it is my responsibility to pay any difference.

☐ My donation does not qualify for Gift Aid.

Please notify BRF if you want to cancel this Gift Aid declaration, change your name or home address, or no longer pay sufficient tax on your income and/or capital gains.

Please complete other side of form ➜

Please return this form to:
BRF, 15 The Chambers, Vineyard, Abingdon OX14 3FE

The Bible Reading Fellowship is a Registered Charity (233280)

SHARING OUR VISION – MAKING A GIFT

Regular giving

By Direct Debit: You can set up a Direct Debit quickly and easily at **brf.org.uk/donate**

By Standing Order: Please contact our Fundraising Administrator +44 (0)1865 319700 | **giving@brf.org.uk**

One-off donation

Please accept my gift of:

☐ £10 ☐ £50 ☐ £100 Other £ _____

by (*delete as appropriate*):

☐ Cheque/Charity Voucher payable to 'BRF'

☐ MasterCard/Visa/Debit card/Charity card

Name on card

Card no. ☐☐☐☐ ☐☐☐☐☐☐ ☐☐☐☐☐ ☐☐☐☐

Expires end ☐M☐M ☐Y☐Y Security code* ☐☐☐

*Last 3 digits on the reverse of the card
ESSENTIAL IN ORDER TO PROCESS YOUR PAYMENT

Signature   Date

☐ I would like to leave a gift in my will to BRF.

For more information, visit **brf.org.uk/lastingdifference**

For help or advice regarding making a gift, please contact our Fundraising Administrator +44 (0)1865 319700

☚ Please complete other side of form

Please return this form to:
BRF, 15 The Chambers, Vineyard, Abingdon OX14 3FE

BRF

The Bible Reading Fellowship is a Registered Charity (233280)

GL0319

GUIDELINES SUBSCRIPTION RATES

Please note our new subscription rates, current until 30 April 2020:

Individual subscriptions
covering 3 issues for under 5 copies, payable in advance
(including postage & packing):

	UK	Europe	Rest of world
Guidelines 1-year subscription	£17.40	£25.50	£29.40
Guidelines 3-year subscription (9 issues)	£49.50	N/A	N/A

Group subscriptions
covering 3 issues for 5 copies or more, sent to one UK address (post free):

Guidelines 1-year subscription	£13.80 per set of 3 issues p.a.

Please note that the annual billing period for group subscriptions runs from 1 May to 30 April.

Overseas group subscription rates
Available on request. Please email **enquiries@brf.org.uk**.

Copies may also be obtained from Christian bookshops:

Guidelines	£4.60 per copy

All our Bible reading notes can be ordered
online by visiting **biblereadingnotes.org.uk/
subscriptions**

GUIDELINES

Guidelines is also available as
an app for Android, iPhone and iPad
biblereadingnotes.org.uk/apps

GUIDELINES INDIVIDUAL SUBSCRIPTION FORM

All our Bible reading notes can be ordered online by visiting
biblereadingnotes.org.uk/subscriptions

☐ I would like to take out a subscription:

Title .... First name/initials .... Surname ....

Address ....

.... Postcode ....

Telephone .... Email ....

Please send *Guidelines* beginning with the January 2020 / May 2020 / September
2020 issue (*delete as appropriate*):

(*please tick box*)

	UK	Europe	Rest of world
Guidelines 1-year subscription	☐ £17.40	☐ £25.50	☐ £29.40
Guidelines 3-year subscription	☐ £49.50	N/A	N/A

Total enclosed £ .... (cheques should be made payable to 'BRF')

Please charge my MasterCard / Visa ☐ Debit card ☐ with £ ....

Card no. ☐☐☐☐ ☐☐☐☐ ☐☐☐☐ ☐☐☐☐

Expires end ☐☐ ☐☐   Security code* ☐☐☐   Last 3 digits on the reverse
of the card

Signature* .... Date ...... /...... /......

*ESSENTIAL IN ORDER TO PROCESS YOUR PAYMENT

To set up a Direct Debit, please also complete the Direct Debit instruction
on page 159 and return it to BRF with this form.

Please return this form to:
BRF, 15 The Chambers, Vineyard, Abingdon OX14 3FE

To read our terms and find out about cancelling your order, please visit **brfonline.org.uk/terms**.

The Bible Reading Fellowship (BRF) is a Registered Charity (233280)

GL0319

GUIDELINES GIFT SUBSCRIPTION FORM

☐ I would like to give a gift subscription (please provide both names and addresses):

Title .... First name/initials .... Surname ....

Address ....

.... Postcode ....

Telephone .... Email ....

Gift subscription name ....

Gift subscription address ....

.... Postcode ....

Gift message (20 words max. or include your own gift card):

....

....

Please send *Guidelines* beginning with the January 2020 / May 2020 / September 2020 issue (*delete as appropriate*):

(please tick box)	UK	Europe	Rest of world
Guidelines 1-year subscription	☐ £17.40	☐ £25.50	☐ £29.40
Guidelines 3-year subscription	☐ £49.50	N/A	N/A

Total enclosed £ .... (cheques should be made payable to 'BRF')

Please charge my MasterCard / Visa ☐ Debit card ☐ with £ ....

Card no. ☐☐☐☐ ☐☐☐☐ ☐☐☐☐ ☐☐☐☐ · ☐☐☐

Expires end ☐☐ ☐☐   Security code* ☐☐☐   Last 3 digits on the reverse of the card

Signature* .... Date ...... / ...... / ......

*ESSENTIAL IN ORDER TO PROCESS YOUR PAYMENT

To set up a Direct Debit, please also complete the Direct Debit instruction on page 159 and return it to BRF with this form.

Please return this form to:
BRF, 15 The Chambers, Vineyard, Abingdon OX14 3FE

To read our terms and find out about cancelling your order, please visit **brfonline.org.uk/terms**.

The Bible Reading Fellowship (BRF) is a Registered Charity (233280)

DIRECT DEBIT PAYMENT

You can pay for your annual subscription to our Bible reading notes using Direct Debit. You need only give your bank details once, and the payment is made automatically every year until you cancel it. If you would like to pay by Direct Debit, please use the form opposite, entering your BRF account number under 'Reference number'.

You are fully covered by the Direct Debit Guarantee:

The Direct Debit Guarantee

- This Guarantee is offered by all banks and building societies that accept instructions to pay Direct Debits.
- If there are any changes to the amount, date or frequency of your Direct Debit, The Bible Reading Fellowship will notify you 10 working days in advance of your account being debited or as otherwise agreed. If you request The Bible Reading Fellowship to collect a payment, confirmation of the amount and date will be given to you at the time of the request.
- If an error is made in the payment of your Direct Debit, by The Bible Reading Fellowship or your bank or building society, you are entitled to a full and immediate refund of the amount paid from your bank or building society.
- If you receive a refund you are not entitled to, you must pay it back when The Bible Reading Fellowship asks you to.
- You can cancel a Direct Debit at any time by simply contacting your bank or building society. Written confirmation may be required. Please also notify us.

The Bible Reading Fellowship

Instruction to your bank or building society to pay by Direct Debit

Please fill in the whole form using a ballpoint pen and return it to:
BRF, 15 The Chambers, Vineyard, Abingdon OX14 3FE

Service User Number: | 5 | 5 | 8 | 2 | 2 | 9 |

Name and full postal address of your bank or building society

To: The Manager	Bank/Building Society
Address	
	Postcode

Name(s) of account holder(s)

Branch sort code

| | | - | | | - | | |

Bank/Building Society account number

Reference number

Instruction to your Bank/Building Society
Please pay The Bible Reading Fellowship Direct Debits from the account detailed in this instruction, subject to the safeguards assured by the Direct Debit Guarantee. I understand that this instruction may remain with The Bible Reading Fellowship and, if so, details will be passed electronically to my bank/building society.

Signature(s)

Banks and Building Societies may not accept Direct Debit instructions for some types of account.